From POVERTY to PROSPERITY

A Collection of Stories About the Power to Change

by

Alfreda Bradford

From POVERTY to PROSPERITY

A Collection of Stories About the Power to Change

by

Alfreda Bradford

ANOINTED ROSE PRESS™

The Anointed Rose Press name and logo are registered Trademarks
ANOINTED ROSE PRESS™ PUBLISHING

From Poverty to Prosperity©
The Power to Change

ALFREDA BRADFORD
Email: bradfordalfreda@gmail.com
Website: AlfredaBradford.com
(267) 719-3386

ISBN-13: 978-0=9896110-1-5
ISBN-10: 0-9896110-1-9
©2014 by Alfreda Bradford

Anointed Rose Press: Coatesville, PA 19320
Email: anointed.rose.press@gmail.com

Library of Congress Control Number: 2014945153
Library of Congress Catalog-in-Publication Data

Bradford, Alfreda
From Poverty to Prosperity: The Power to Change / Alfreda Bradford
p.cm.

ISBN 978-0-9896110-1-5 (trade pbk.: alk. Paper)

08 09 10 11 12 13 14   AnR LS   10 9 8 7 6 5 4 3 2 1

1. Religion: Christian Life Inspirational   2. Biography and Autobiography: Personal Memoirs

Cover Design: Kingdom Innovative Prints (267) 625-0308

All materials on these pages are copyrighted by Alfreda Bradford, unless otherwise indicated. All rights reserved. No part of these pages, either text or image may be used for any purpose other than personal use. Therefore, reproduction, modification, storage in a retrieval system or retransmission, in any form or by any means, electronic, mechanical or otherwise, for reasons other than personal use, is strictly prohibited without prior written permission.
Unless otherwise indicated, all Scripture quotations are taken from the King James Version.
Printed in the USA for worldwide distribution.

Dedication Page

This book is dedicated to my dearly beloved Mother, Pastor Evelyn H. Westfield, whose example of true love and commitment has inspired me to never quit and to keep on moving.

The expression of my heart's desire for my three beautiful daughters, Tanisha, Erika and Nia, for them to live a life beyond their expectations, which have birthed many dreams in me and still I continue.

My lovely granddaughters Whitney and Myah; twin grandson's Ayden and Ethyn, that they will never be forced to repeat the darkness this family has experienced but instead flow in the ocean of light and generational blessings and perpetual increase.

Alfreda

Acknowledgements

I am grateful to those who have assisted me in making this dream a reality. Special thanks to all of the following people— my publisher, September Summer, who stepped in and pulled everything together in a most timely and professional fashion; Paulette Gray who has assisted me to more fully communicate my thoughts to writing; and Sarah J. Flashing whose sacrifices and sincere willingness to see me succeed in my endeavors, was expressed in her continual expressions of going over and beyond the call of duty.

To all of the Contributors who I interviewed for their collections; Carmelo Colon, Jr., J.B. Tremont, Tonya Patterson, Letitia Alexander, Tanya Norwood, Shawntrell Sherrod, Dr. Inetta Jenkins-Cooper, and Peter Edwin.

To my Bishop, Rev. Eric A. Lambert, Jr., whose continual rich outpouring of the teachings of the Holy Scriptures has pulled me up and kept me on track.

And most of all, to my three greatest friends—God the Father, God the Son and God the Holy Spirit.

Alfreda Bradford

Foreword

Beloved, I wish above all things that thou mayest prosper and be in health, even as thy soul prospereth.
3 John 1:2 (KJV)

These words reflect the heart of God. He wants His children to be successful and prosper in whatever they put their hands to do. I know that success is a key component of the Kingdom of God, and we must make every effort to see that success becomes ours.
In her book, "From Poverty to Prosperity", Alfreda Bradford uses life applicable lessons to encourage others to make the transition from a defeated, non-productive life, to one that resonates with the blessings of God.

This book uses various success stories to motivate the reader to move onward and upward in their quest for success. There are many who equate poverty with Christianity, yet I do not believe that poverty is the will of God for humanity. I have known Alfreda for many years and I have watched her passion for creating success for herself, grow to include making others successful. Alfreda does this with excellence and a spirit of faith.

Alfreda has compiled many short stories to let the reader know that the Lord is still working on behalf of those who trust Him. I am sure that you will find comfort and encouragement in the stories that you read.

From Poverty to Prosperity is indeed a book that everyone needs to have in their personal libraries, and I trust you will join me in making the lessons of this book your lessons for life.
Peace and blessings to all.

Bishop Eric A. Lambert, Jr
Bethel Deliverance International Church
2901 W. Cheltenham Ave.
Wyncote, PA 19095

Foreword

This book, a compilation of stories of individual's lives, their journeys, failures and triumph wonderfully unfold the processes necessary to achieve temporal and spiritual success.

These are the stories of people who over time learned what's important and what's not; and some instances of who matters, and who shouldn't have, and who matters most.

These stories help you think about your own story, what you've come through, and the continual unfolding of God's perfect plan for all our lives.

Someone once said that there is nothing that beats failure like success. These real life stories help us all to understand better, the process.

Dr. Leonard Robinson
Pastor, Kingdom Vision Ministries International

Dedication…vi

Acknowledgements…viii

Foreword…ix

Foreword…xi

Table of Contents

Introduction…xv

Prelude…xvii

Chapter 1 | She Was Me…1
Alfreda Bradford

Chapter 2 | Don't Be A Fool…32
Tonya Patterson

Chapter 3 | The Love of a Mother…39
Letitia Alexander

Chapter 4 | The Lord is Good!...47
Tanya Norwood

Chapter 5 | Love Sought Me Out and Brought Me Out…51
Shawntell Sherrod

Chapter 6 | To Be Continued…71
Dr. Inetta J Cooper

Chapter 7 | Transforming Grace…76
Carmelo Colon, Jr.

Chapter 8 | Pursuing Joy & Prosperity…82
Brother Peter Edwin

Chapter 9 | Knowing your Purpose…97
J.B. Tremont

Chapter 10 | Synopsis…112
Alfreda Bradford

Appendix

Salvation…115

About the Author…119

About the Contributors…121

Introduction

This is a collection of stories about blessings from God, and the power to change during trial and crisis. The world would be a different place if more of us would take the time and energy to encourage our neighbors by sharing our personal stories. The truth of the matter is that we all have a story. Sometimes we envy successful people when we see their glory, neglecting to remember that they, too, have a story. We begin at one point in life, and through a series of events and the choices we make, and/or choices that others made for us; we have arrived at our present state of time and circumstances.

All of the contributors of this book, "From Poverty to Prosperity: The Power to Change," have had different experiences though we hold one main thing in common. We know that regardless of your history, failures, traumas and fears Jesus will meet you where you are and erase your pain away.

We write to empower you. You do not have to remain in a state of un-forgiveness or full of fear. You don't have to remain sick, stuck, broken, sad, mad, depressed, busted and disgusted. We become new creatures when we exercise faith to accept Jesus Christ in our hearts as Lord and Savior (2 Cor. 5:17). Immediately thereafter, your past experiences hold absolutely no weight or power to dictate your present and future status and outcome in God's eternal Kingdom, which is now!

We pray that these brief stories will be sufficient to meet your need, soften your heart, and bring you hope and knowledge in knowing that you are not alone. Others are in the same, or worse, situations, and there is nothing too hard for God to do. Man's extremity is God's opportunity to work.

Enjoy,
Alfreda B.

Prelude

Sitting in a semi-dark cave all alone, with kneecaps folded to shoulders, and arms wrapped around knees; I was getting old with apparent grayness. I could look out from my partial position but to find me, you previously had to seek for me or know that I was there.

It was a lonely place. Why was I hiding? Where was everyone else? How did I get there? What was I waiting for? What was I thinking? How was I feeling? Did me stumble across me or was it a divine appointment? Who is she? Who is me? How did I become she? Where was me all the time? How did me find she? Where did she go? What happens to me now?

One day I had a visitor, and the visitor was me. Me touched me without stretched hands. Me had come to visit and pray for me. I felt her strong and determined touch. I was empowered by it. I was able to rise, leave my bed and run for my life. I have not been the same from that day forth.

Who is she? SHE IS ME!

A Ride to Remember

It was a happy day. I sat in the back of this fancy car with my sister. My biological father was in the driver's seat with someone else as a front passenger, whose face was unknown. My legs were swinging very swiftly as I sang the words of a happy song. This is the only childhood experience I remember of my father. Maybe because it was the Christmas season, my mother allowed the two of us to go with him on this particular day. We departed from my other siblings. At the time, I knew he was my father; even though, I do not recall any previous encounters with him.

The drive was not too far. I remember my fancy socks, and feeling good about myself as I sat all dressed up very girly, like a doll baby. When we reached our destination, I continued to sit in the car. I can vividly recall my father and She walking into the entrance of what appeared to be a hotel.

It's now been fifty years or more, and She still has not returned from that hotel. She is still missing, and no one has reported her gone. Where is She? Where did She go? Why did She go? When will She come home?

This was the day that She was kidnapped from me. Our acquaintance was new. We had not been together long enough. I enjoyed her company. She was fun, and made me feel good to be with her, but who was She? Where was She? I think I might have become a little anxious when I thought about her. I did not think about her often because I eventually dismissed her, or so I thought.

In the process of spiritual growth and development, I write this book having recently discovered, and openly confessing, exactly who She was. She was my Innocence.

Where She Was

I do not know what happened to her in that hotel room. She has not reached out to me to communicate a word or a signal. I am left only to wonder. I was forced to move forward in life without her. I miss her dearly, and I am not completely happy without her. My life is unfulfilled and incomplete with her not being there. She was the source of my life, my laughter, and my joy. I was robbed. A part of me was destroyed. Why did this happen to me?

Today I cry. I needed to cry. Nothing or no other experience in life has seemed to impact me to this level of tears prior to this. It's been a long time coming, and I thank God for it. I grew up knowing that something was not quite right, and that something was missing in my life. She was gone, but I didn't know She should have been with Me. After all, I was only around the age of 8 when She was taken away.

I couldn't put my hands on the missing components in my life. However, my natural instincts revealed such things to me. Was there more to life? Of course, there had to be! Actually, She was forced and blocked out of my memory. In some type of mystical way, I knew She was supposed to be with me, but yet She was not. My history revealed her absence; indicated by the numerous starting and not finishing of processes in my life. There are too many to count!

In retrospect, we were both lonely and afraid. The only difference is, She was hiding and tucked away on the inside. I grew up as an introvert, hiding. But on the outside, I was forced by the gravity of life and the motivations of others to move forward. So, I somehow covered up her memory as I went.

My grief is too much to bear, and has been hidden and built up over the years, without a healthy outlet. Until now, I have never discussed She with anyone. To my knowledge, I am the only one who had an opportunity to meet her, other than those who have been graced with a special gift of discernment. If per chance someone else knew her or saw her in hiding, they have yet to mention it to me. Today, I finally get a chance to release. Today I cry.

I Returned to the Hotel

I cry, yet, my tears contain a twofold purpose. At the same time, I cry a cry of release and one of joy as I have recently been reacquainted with She. It was a long trip. I walked confidently alone as I strode down a fairly long, well lit corridor. It was a quiet trip other than some last minute drama taking place next door. But I did not let it stop me; I kept on moving. I don't know how I knew I was at the right place, but somehow I did. When I arrived at the door, the door was closed but unlocked. I remember saying to myself, as I turned the doorknob, to remind my daughter to keep the doors locked.

I entered into the room. It was very neat, orderly, clean, breezy, and well lit. The bathroom was the first room to the left. I peeked into the room and looked around to see who was there; or who lived there. At first, I did not see anyone. I don't know what made me shut and lock the door, even placing the security chain on it. Moments later, just before She made her appearance, I noticed the chains were broken and laying on the floor. Yet the door remained shut. How did this happen? Who broke the chains? I looked up again, and there She was.

She was moving gracefully in my direction, becoming clearer and clearer. It was almost as if She was appearing from the past to the present. My mouth was opened. I was amazed. She has never spoken an audible word to me. Matter of fact, She has not spoken to anyone since that devastating night. I had no contact with her, and I did not know that it was She until I saw her. It was as if I was looking in a mirror. We were identical twins. I knew it was Me. I still remember the pretty, bright yellow outfit she wore. She didn't stop. She kept coming. SHE WAS ME.

She had been there in that room all the time, for 50 years now; locked up, isolated, sheltered, clean, orderly, beautiful, and glowing but alone. I was overpowered by her presence, her smile and her glory.

She was me but She was more than Me. I am not sure who introduced themselves first, She or Me. Regardless, it was a very satisfying and immediate reunion of spirit, soul, mind and body. It was a sweet reconnection and complete inner awareness. I AM NOW SHE, and SHE IS ME. We are one again.

Where was She all this time? I don't know, but I would like to. She has not revealed anything to me as of yet; I have no details from her. I have no idea what She did in that hotel room for the last 50 years (the "hotel" room was actually a room in my inner man).

Over the years, every now and then I could surmise (even though I did not know what it was at the time) the piercing of her eyes watching me as She quickly glanced out of her peeping hole, looking into life through my windows. However, She did not look far, and She did not look long. Her eyes would only look at me, and then She would drift back into seclusion again.

I have been made whole, total, and complete by the reunion with She. Oh, what a holy reunion. We have places to go and we are on our way. My closest point of reference is the similarity to that of a home reunion. All of the incomplete goals and unfinished projects over the years have been revisited, brushed off, picked up, and carried to completion. This is possible now all because She is back - back with Me. The genuine restoration of purity, innocence, concern, joy, laughter, peace, purpose, increase, and prosperity have all returned. There is no stopping me now.

The Secret of Restoration

How did I find She? How did I get control? How did I locate her? Where did I get the address? How did I get there? Who showed me which way to go? How long did it take for me to locate her? Who prayed for me, guided me, supported me, covered me, protected me, and lifted me; and who paid the fare?

Is this considered a miracle? You bet your bottom dollar it is. We all know that people are dying every day without answers and solutions. She and He have departed from other individuals as young people, even younger than at my experience; who have not and who will not return. But, She was returned to Me.

Well, I honestly confess that it was a process of events that had to unfold. I may never know all the people to thank for the prayers they sent up for me, but there is one Person I know of for sure. He happens to be my very best friend. His names are Jehovah Rophi, my Healer; Jehovah Yireh, my Provider; Jehovah Nissi, my Banner; Jehovah Shalom, my Peace; Jehovah Roi, my Shepherd and Jehovah Tsidkenu, my Righteousness. He is Jesus, the Lily of the Valley, and the Bright and Morning Star. He is my Lord and my Saviour.

During and after a tedious and suffering process, I began to experience Divine Deliverance. Due to my stubbornness and reluctance to live the way God wanted me to, these Deliverances did not take place all at one time. They were manifested in layers. Finally, when I was ready, God was ready. The time was right and it happened. There was no chance of this happening prematurely. Matter of fact, I didn't even know what I was seeking. I was finally and sincerely at the point of life where the only person I sought and lived for was God. He is absolutely first. He is God. He is King.

I am now a true Christian in my heart, with no hypocrisy. Above all else, I have presented my body as a living sacrifice, holy and acceptable to the Lord, which is my reasonable service; no longer conformed by the world but transformed by the renewing of my mind, therefore, proving the good, perfect and acceptable will of God (Romans 12:1-2) striving to walk in total obedience.

I have sold myself completely out to Him in that He is now able to do whatever He needs to do with me, whenever He desires to do it. He has prepared me for His purposes and services, and I am ready to serve. It was not easy, but it has taken place. Hallelujah, it has come to pass!
I LOVE JESUS!

Chapter 1 / She Was Me

Alfreda Bradford

In love, I open my life, and write in this book to encourage others—especially women— that you can absolutely arise and abound in every area of your life, regardless of experiences or history—past or present.

I thank my daughters for their selflessness—for sharing me with pen and paper as I engrossed myself with thought. I engaged myself within myself in order to produce a new self, ME!

To my lovely Mother, whose life of virtue and integrity—intertwined with the love of God—has caused me to create a desire to be the same.

I have unspeakable gratitude to my previous and present editor, Paulette Gray and Sarah Flashing, respectively. I surrendered myself on paper into their hands and they handled the sensitivity with extreme delicate care. They worked very diligently to give order and conformity to affirm that you, the reader, would be able to comprehend. Last, but actually first, I thank God who has always been with me. It is through His divine and awesome love, mercy, grace, provisions, compassion and power that I am what I am; and I am already what I shall become. I know love because He is!

What Made Me Cry

I was born and raised in poverty. Even on the lowest level, I always had the necessities of life. The firstborn of seven children, I was raised with six sisters in a tiny three bedroom, and roach infested row house. My mother and my stepfather had the front bedroom, and I shared the back room with my second born sister. Our bedroom faced the old cemetery. I was 12 years old around the time that we moved into the house. Prior to that, we moved a lot—at least once a year that I could recall. We had no working TV but I remember listening to the radio on occasion; and I used my imagination a lot. I had no idea how much of a blessing this would be later on in life, as I would use my creative skills to bring things from the invisible into the visible.

While growing up, there was not much to do. We walked to the corner store or to the laundromat; or we sat on the steps and played cleaners, where one of us would bring our dirty clothes to the other. One would write up a receipt, and one would pick up the same dirty clothes a little later.

I have vivid memories of being 6 years old, and my mother dropping me off at school the first day—I cried my little heart out. *"Mommy, please? Please come back!"* I hardly had any time with her. I can only remember being alone, as a child, with my mother three times. Once when I was about 7 years old, I was fortunate enough to have lunch alone with her at the corner deli. The second time happened when I brought home a good report card. The third time was when I faked taking some pills. I told my mother, and she took me to the hospital. I did not care. I had her all to myself.

So many people in our house needed attention, and there was hardly time for me. At the hospital, we were away from the crowd. It was just us. I wanted more of the private parties, and more time with mommy. She had always been there physically, but I needed a mental connection. I felt lonely and disconnected. I will never forget the encouraging words she spoke when she told me how smart I was. I had gotten good grades at school. Her beautiful face is etched in my mind. Subconsciously, I have strived for a repeat of that day. I wanted to hear those words again. I was inwardly seeking mom's approval and encouragement.

Where was my father in all of this? It was rumored that my father lived in the same city. However, I had not seen him since I spent a Christmas with him and my sister in what I believe was a hotel. The lights were shining. Everything around us was sparkly and beautiful. My sister and I were very young, and it would be another thirty years before I would see him again.

I adjusted to the crowd by withdrawing from it. I learned to be alone even when I was not alone. I isolated myself from within. I was a lonely little girl in a house overflowing with people. I had no one to talk to me. I wanted my mommy. I wanted my daddy. I wanted acknowledgement. Somebody touch me please! Please step into my world; I need a friend.

Mother was having babies every year, and getting up early to go to work every day. In between, she was out of the house seeking a real break from all the people. I was the oldest child, and I paid a price when things were not right. There were no breaks for me.

What Made Me Love?

I grew up quite ignorant, with no clue to the meaning of life. I had no idea how babies were conceived or born; or how money was accumulated. I didn't know how the rich were rich or how the poor were poor. I was lost in a world that seemed against me. Why? I had no one talking to me, mentoring me, instructing me or speaking into my life. My step-dad did not communicate with me, and my mom was young and busy with all of my siblings.

Left to myself—in a world all to myself—I communicated with myself quite often. I fantasized frequently and created my own illusions. I credit my thinking abilities to these events. It was think or die. I was emotionally destitute.

Back to the topic of love! David (who we will talk more about later) often told me on several occasions that I had a problem receiving love. As I reflect on his words, I know now he was absolutely correct. I could not recognize love because I had no reference for it. What was love? One would think that if someone loved them, they would talk to them. But no one was talking to me; not in a way that was substantial. No one was there to help guide me in places of importance; the knowledgeable places that could help to shape and guide my efforts in doing well. In my mind, sex became love. How very wrong I was.

I did not know many men intimately — all of my relationships were long term. I thought that was another form of love. I thought that if you loved someone, you stayed in spite of the circumstances; whether married or not. I had been in one intimate relationship with the father of my eldest daughter but intimacy was not something that I was familiar with. Maybe if things had been different in my life, love would have come with a different perspective.

Did I marry for love? What was love—sex? We had very little of that after I figured out how to do it. We married in August of 1973, because I had given birth to a beautiful baby girl in February of that year. It was the right thing to do. Needless to say, however, the marriage lasted about a year. What a shame! He was, and is, a wonderful and beautiful human being. He is a great father to his daughter.

Nevertheless, we did not last. With both of us being young and naive, we allowed infidelity to separate us.

Eight years later, I met a single man and tried marriage again. Surely, it would work this time because of all that had transpired in my life; especially since I had given my life to Christ and experienced God's gracious forgiveness. Saved and twenty-five years old, I was striving to live for Christ. I attempted to walk a chalk line and live a chaste life for a three year period. I was hot! My hormones were jumping, and I did not know what to do with myself.

It did not matter that David was thirteen years older than I. He was tall, handsome and interested in me. Our relationship developed quickly, but I didn't know this man as well as I should have. He did not even have a job at the time. He was my stepfather's cousin and had relocated from Cleveland, Tennessee to Philadelphia. He was the new kid on the block.

I had a house, so getting married to have sex seemed to be the logical next step. Needless to say, that was a very bad decision. Prior to his salvation, my husband was an alcoholic. I later found out that he abused his former wife on several occasions. However, I did not take the time to find out why this took place. Even if I knew, I probably would have still married him because I wanted to have sex within the bounds of marriage. I desired a sex life that came without condemnation, but I was not prepared for the mental abuse I suffered.

We were married for five years before the children were born. I remember sitting on the back porch holding the girls and praying that they would not marry anyone who came close to the crazy man that I had to have. I had confused sex for love—or was it love for sex? Whatever, it was not right.

In a strange way, I believe I should have taken heed to one of my mother's friends, a pastor, who stopped by before our wedding. He tried to tell me not to marry David without trying out the sex first. I thought his advice was strange and certainly against the grain of God's word. A man of God telling me to have sex before marriage was unheard of!

I shared the pastor's thoughts with David, and he agreed with me. We did not advocate sex before marriage. In retrospect, I wish I had taken the risk. I regretted my marriage in that I spent 13 years in a union without intimate sexual fulfillment. Yet, God's will was done and two gorgeous girls were conceived out of the union. David and I were both saved, was that not enough?

> *That if thou shalt confess with thy mouth the Lord Jesus, and shalt believe in thine heart that God hath raised him from the dead, thou shalt be saved. (Romans 9:10)*

No! It was not enough. Just because two people are saved does not automatically put them on the same accord. We were not compatible in other important ways. I guess he strived to please me sexually but I was starving mentally. I got what I asked for and more, just as I thought I wanted — a penis with a man attached. But, sexual satisfaction escaped me in this relationship. Still I never had any sexual relationship outside of my marriage to him. We were married, but I was empty. The marriage deteriorated from less to "minus less". I went back to the place I knew well. I had lived this before at an address, in a bed, living in the shell I created to keep others out.

What Made Me Sick?

I gave birth to three beautiful daughters. There are sixteen years between the first and the second one; and I carried them well. The first was born on the exact due date—two days prior to Valentine's Day, though I still consider her to be my Valentine baby. The second was born 6 weeks early. Due in the middle of August, she was born one day before Independence Day—she is my firecracker baby. The third baby did not want to come out. She was due November 8, but labor was induced on November 27, the Friday after Thanksgiving. She is my Thanksgiving baby.

The last baby was the only one that took any effort to birth; but I was extremely sick with all of them. I suffered severe nausea, indigestion and spitting. That's right—spitting. I could not control my saliva. I walked around with a can so I could spit in it as the saliva perpetually built up. If I chewed gum, the water increased. Though they did a number of tests, the doctors didn't have a clue what was happening. I determined that I was not going to continue to take pills, lotions and potions that gave no relief.

I would place a towel on the bed pillow to catch the saliva as I slept. I was glad to eat food, but as soon as I swallowed the last bite, the saliva would immediately build up again; not to mention that most of the time, the food would come back up also. "What's the purpose of eating?" I would ask my doctor. "Well, at least the body would get the nutrients, even though it may have only held it for about three minutes."

On many occasions, I would have my head in the toilet vomiting, spitting and urinating on myself all at the same time because my bladder was weak. It was truly a season of hope. I stayed positive because I knew that the day would come when it would all be over. But, with the risk of miscarriage, I was confined to bed rest for the last 5 months with my last daughter. I was told to walk on my knees when it was time to go into the bathroom.

What Was Next?

Eventually, I was without male companionship for some time because my husband died from cancer. It is difficult to observe the descent into the place that cancer takes the ones you love.

Time passed and a friend introduced me to a man. Ironically, this friend was interested in me as more than a friend and so was the new man. The new man won. He introduced me to a world of mortgages and to him. He provided high interest rates, outrageous broker points and personal satisfaction. I was hooked on him *and* on making money through the mortgage industry. This was not a good time in my life. I compromised on my values.

We became intimately involved. I gave him what he wanted in business; and at home he gave me what I needed. His specialty was women, women, and more women. I allowed myself to be drawn into an ungodly relationship with a man who had too many other women. I later found out about his many other involvements, and allowed him to beg and plead with me to give him full reign to be with the other girl. I knew better. My self-esteem was so broken. He knew I was vulnerable and manipulated me.

Although I wanted the other lady and, possibly more, women out of the way; he talked me into me being his main woman. I agreed and the others would be his supplemental interests. I played myself. I did not like it. I really wanted all or nothing. When was all this going to end? My life was not honoring God. I was a woman who had accepted Jesus Christ as Lord, and now I was a backslider. I was ashamed of what I had done, and knew I had to break off this liaison so I could be made whole.

What Made Me Think?

I finally realized that compromising only brought fleeting satisfaction. One tries to get in the right frame of mind to enjoy oneself, but the guilt is always there. You want the good life—big house, nice cars, fancy clothes, the love of a successful man. Most women dream this same dream.

But, I never really had it in my grasp. Impatience had caused me to cooperate with the devil. I was living a lie to get what I thought I needed—simply because I wanted it. When he was not with me, he was with someone else. He was not my husband, so engaging in sex was out of order because it was totally against the word of God.

I would sometimes justify my behavior by thinking about how long I had been in a sexually unfulfilled marriage. But, my conduct resulted in collateral damage to me and the generations to follow. Everything appears to be fine, and it seems God has granted us immunity. But, the consequences of our ways are reaped at another time.

> *Be not deceived; God is not mocked: whatsoever a man (or woman) sows that shall he/she will also reap. (Galatians 6:7) NKJV*

Yielding to the gratification of the flesh instead of waiting for God is a slap in the face of a loving and sovereign Lord. What looks like a dilemma to us is God's opportune time to teach and prepare. I wanted and needed forgiveness so I could move on to the new places God was going to take me. Because he promised forgiveness, grace and mercy were sure to follow. That is what the word of God says.

Calling on the Lord, and a measured dose of retrospection made me see what I did and did not need in my life. What happened? I compromised. I had not allowed my life to be led by the Spirit. My success to the real extent was overthrown, and to what point? How did the word of God line up in the mess I had created? I was saved and I knew better. How can two walk together unless they agree? Take inventory of whom you associate. If their walk is not in line with godliness, it would be to your benefit to leave them to themselves and pray for them.

What Made Me Laugh?

Freedom! Thank God for freedom. Freedom of the soul and spirit was wonderful. I rediscovered and more importantly, reconnected with the lover of my soul. I vowed not to run out on him again. I was torn between two lovers—the world and the love of God. I made a decision to sow to the Spirit. I would do what was necessary in order to live a righteous life.

This process came with a deep soul searching, and the help from God. I will never forget the day I asked God to show me myself the way He sees me. When He answered my prayer, I had to ask God who He was talking about. Then, I realized it was me. I repented until I reached the point of forgiving myself for the secreted wickedness in my heart. Since that time, I have positioned myself in a state of continual prayer, repentance and fasting. No, I am not on my knees all day long, but I am in the Spirit all day. I pray to God with a sincere heart.

Prayer is simply communication with God. If you are born again and have confessed the sins in your life, God will hear and He will answer. It is a new found restoration—the joy of the Lord, the freedom of the Spirit—no condemnation or guilt knowing that we are forgiven, and that judgment is erased. I begin everyday with God in prayer. I spend time in his Word, being quiet enough to listen to what He desires to say to me. It is this peace of mind and soul that allows the healing waters of life to flow through me and toward others. Imagine peace with yourself. You can laugh at yourself, laugh with yourself, and laugh with others. I laugh now for I am at peace with myself, and laughter is made easy.

What Made Me Whole?

The devil comes to steal, kill and destroy (John 10:10). Jesus comes that we might have life and have it more abundantly. We seek to be made whole in him. Wholeness represents the attainment of right mind, body, spirit, finances and relationships. We need to be healed. We have many wounds, some self-inflicted and some not. Some scars we have are carried for a lifetime. Some of us have mental abuse and disorders, physical handicaps and spiritual deficiencies. We live beneath our privilege. We live way below our intent.

We are in poverty when we are without any substantial relationship with anyone for any appreciable time. We do not care or even know ourselves and are sometimes convinced we do not like ourselves. But, Jesus is our Healer. We cover up painful memories in our subconscious mind. There are tears, wounds, and events of the past that are too hurtful and heavy to remember. They are covered but they remain. When you sweep the trash under the rug, you cannot see it but the lack of a smooth surface will become more evident as time goes on.

You have to let God into your heart so He can have control and fix the broken pieces. His Spirit gets to the root of the matter and digs up the residue in your soul. Confession and forgiveness prepare us for the harvest that comes when we plant seeds of righteousness. When the child of God has done wrong, she can always pray, ask to be forgiven, accept His forgiveness and start anew. But, He is more than Savior of circumstances. He is Lord—the Sovereign of the Universe.

What Made Me Push?

I had to learn to push past procrastination. Procrastination has destroyed more than its share of "would be" successes. I have accomplishments as well. I have completed 31 continuous years in Real Estate, and 29 years in ministry as an Evangelist. I have achieved a U.S. patent for my shovel invention, and have raised three beautiful daughters. One daughter is a successful hair stylist, and has also worked with me in the real estate industry for a few years. She has been married in excess of 13 years, and is raising my two strikingly beautiful and talented granddaughters. I thank God for her.

Another daughter is in college. She is super talented with creative juices that flow toward design—fashion and web. See her work and you will wonder why she goes to school, for her talents are obvious. She has just launched her own business and has always known what she wanted to do. She has never needed a plan B because she's known how to make plan A happen despite all circumstances.

But things have not always been stable. At one point, we were evicted from our house and our family was separated—the two youngest were at my oldest daughter's house, and I was sleeping on the couch at my mother's house. All during that time, my daughter was continuing in school, traveling back and forth forty-five minutes to an hour on public transportation. That lasted for two months. Today, she is also an Evangelist.

My youngest was a senior in high school. An honors student from the time she entered first grade, she has always been a gifted student. She never had to work very hard because her intelligence is natural. Whatever she decides about her vocation, no doubt she will be a success. The world is her oyster. She is a year younger than all her peers, yet well ahead of the pack.

We owe an incredible gift of thanks to the school administrator who made a decision to allow my daughter to enter school even though she missed the age cutoff for that year. She never had a hard time and was never behind at anytime in her learning process. For a while during our time of displacement, the school she attended gave her tokens to travel back and forth to school, and on occasion transported her as well. They gave us a large amount of food and helped us tremendously when we needed it most. All of our needs were met. It was crazy, yet powerful.

We have been through so much together. We are all stronger for the struggles. I wanted them to have the best education so I was willing to pay for it. But, it came at a high price. I fought hard to keep them in the suburbs, but I was living much too high and above my means. There were no car payments or credit card worries, but I just could not afford the monthly expenses as they were. We were always short. You know who your true friends are when you really need help. Some even acted as though they were happy to see us in that position. I remember how unkind they were, but I have nothing in my heart but forgiveness for them.

I asked God not to let my children suffer for the choices I made, and allow me to bear the consequences alone. It was a silly prayer yet not impossible. However, how could we avoid collateral damage? If the lights go out in the house and I live without electricity, we all have no lights. Can the children walk into their bedrooms, flip the switch and not have the consequences of an unpaid bill? Certainly not.

I am raising soldiers and warriors. They know how to adapt quickly, from one situation to the next. They have overcome anxiety and have lived in the best and worst of conditions. They know how to face trials and dilemmas, and to persist in spite of moving, packing and storing, and then moving again, carrying boxes and furniture. They have experienced laughing and crying at the same time. We did it together. Whom was I raising? Who were these ultra-beautiful, multi-talented, singing, tall, lanky, left- handed girls? What extraordinary responsibility and circumstances they were able to overcome!

I could make my own schedule for the majority of my working life, but I have chosen to be there for my children. I was always home when they arrived from school. I could take them to school if they missed the bus or pick them up. I sheltered them, watching over them closely. I gave them liberty while expecting accountability. I needed the addresses, telephone numbers, and driver's license numbers of the boys they dated. I always spoke to the parents of the boys to make sure we were on the same page. I was protecting my daughter's anointing, even though they were not fully aware of it at the time.

What Pushed Me?

I was tired! I was tired of being tired. I was tired of not paying the rent on time, tired of landlord-tenant court. I was tired of evictions, tired of moving, tired of storage, tired of paying hundreds if not thousands in bank insufficient fees, bounced checks, tired of borrowing money, and tired of not having the money to repay. I was tired of poverty. I was tired, tired, tired. I was tired of trying to win the lottery. I was tired of allowing other people to take me off focus. I was tired of knowing my needs were not met. I was the Kings' Kid. I knew all the scriptures that pertained to wealth and prosperity. I had not yet mastered the strategies to manifest them in my life. Believe me—I was damn sick and tired.

I wanted more than anything to experience success that comes from hard work and right positioning. I had tried other business ventures. Some were successful but some were not. I wanted to triumph in a way I had not experienced, but knew in my heart I could. God had given me what I needed. I was the person whose ordained assignment was to help others achieve their goals. In doing so, I knew God would take care of us. If God be for us, who could be against us? (Romans 8:31)

I thank God for answering prayer. My time of fruitful harvest had finally arrived. I woke up one morning and declared to myself that "if it's to be, it's up to me". The past was over and I was running for my life. No shame, no hindrances, and nothing to lose, it was on. I ran into the water realizing that only a few things could have happened. The water would overtake me, I would swim to my destination or the waters would part. If the waters parted, I would then walk through to the other side. One way or another I was about to find out because I had stepped out.

I envisioned that I would do whatever it took to get my feet wet. No more standing on the banks. I was in it to win it, and there was no stopping me now. Life had caused me to push myself to victory; and to earn money that was sufficient to eliminate debt and live a life I tried to lead by perpetration. Ephesians 3:20 reads "Now unto him who is able to do exceedingly above that which we are able to think or ask, according to the power that works in us." I knew my source and I had the power. I was determined that I would persist until I succeeded.

What Made Me Reach?

I became tired of being tired. I was tired of the same routine. Up and down, down and up, but never any real consistency. I spiraled upwards, but not reaching the top. What was it? Could it have been the company I was keeping?

I attempt to be very conscious of my thoughts and mindset. I have moved towards learning to control my thoughts. I have acquired the spiritual discipline to think about what I desire to think about most of the time. The better question is, "What do I want to think about?" I now know how to control my thoughts more than they control me.

While growing up, I would automatically think first on the negative outcome—negative thinking based on my past influences and experiences. I gave too much attention to what people would say or think about me. I could reach a plateau of positive thinking and remain there until the next wind of adversity blew. Then my thoughts would go from dark to light, light to dark and dark to dark again. It happened frequently. I had an unstable subconscious. Was I a loser or winner? I then had to master treatment for the cause of the matter rather than treating the effects.

Walking closer to God than ever before, I was applying truth to my subconscious and affirming my personal development. Attentively listening to my pastor's sermons, he pointed out that we have to be prayerful and selective in the company we keep. Was the problem my company? It had to be! I had only a few friends. But, I guess they were the wrong few! I was never the person who had lots of friends, male or female. I have acquaintances, partners, employees, and business associates whom I have cultivated relationships with; but, few that I could say I have experienced close friendships with.

I do not include family with this group. However, there was a gentleman in my life who had been shadowing me for quite a while. He had been around for years. It was difficult to get rid of him. He was honoring his word to me when he said he was not going anywhere. Talk about serious! I am glad that we did not marry when our flesh was considering it. I cannot spend too much time with him mainly because his way of thinking and mine does not gel. Don't get me wrong, he is a good guy. He is God-fearing, funny, hard working, faithful, and sincere. He will do anything for me—in spite of him admitting that he was not good enough for me and I could do better.

My faith is so crazy that I must continually check myself to make sure I do not cross the line by calling faith what is really presumption. I have found myself therein on many occasions. As I observed his life, I realized he spends too much time watching dramatic talk shows. I call them "Garbage Talk Shows," garbage going in and garbage coming out. He has all this wasted intelligence and many kind deeds, but this type of daily intake hinders his maximum progress and production.

I was already aware of those family members with whom boundaries were required, so he was the only one left. I was sure God was not separating me from my children, for I am their guardian. There was no one left! I gave it all up, and it was not too difficult once I made up my mind. In full reality, I was travelling alone. Sometimes, I thought it would be just me and my girls. However, God was always in the equation, even when I was not acknowledging his presence.

When I relinquished it all—friends, family, associates and the like—it was all returned to me. I must say that for the first time in my life, I have friends. I have about ten God-given friends. For the first time, I was even comfortable inviting one of them over to my home to discuss business. Those who know me know this is not something I typically do.

What changed? I can honestly say that it was *me* becoming a friend. I yielded to love, so my reward was love, and now I am so very happy. I aggravate people when I respond with "Exceedingly Well!" when asked how I am doing. But regardless of my current state of mind, physical well being, or whatever else might be happening in my life, my answer remains the same. I am able to maintain that mindset because I realize that *my circumstances do not dictate my position.*

I have completed a spiritual, social, and economical transitioning and repositioning. I am walking in the direction of my destiny. I am empowering the multitude as I go! I am empowering them with knowledge, love, empathy, encouragement, power, counseling, ministry, connections, options, opportunities, time, support, prayers, and money. This complete picture is true Wealth!

What Made Me Wealthy?

The answer is faith. I had faith in God's Word and faith in His promises. His Word is His promises, and I had faith in myself. Walk with me for a moment and imagine yourself as a very small, lonely seed buried in the earth all alone. There is nothing but the weight of the earth above you and all around you. You are determined to grow. No one knows that you exist, because you are unseen, essentially invisible. All the while, your roots beneath the earth are expanding every moment of the day. You are expanding by leaps and bounds into the soil of the earth, deeper and stronger. Your foundation is strong, solidly established, and not easily moved.

Yet, no one knows you exist. You are there, very much alive and vibrant but still, unseen. How does the tiny, weightless seed push beyond the weight of the whole world? The answer is, "It does not!" As it submits to the laws of the universe its purpose begins to take hold in a natural progression and unfolds. Its season has come. Just as the tender young plant appears today for the world to see, we can ask where was it yesterday? People will say the same thing about you.

Now we can see, feel, smell and touch the beautiful plant. It continues to be nourished by water and sunshine. It remains and abounds. Over time, the plant is manifesting into a garden—a tree and has now pioneered a forest—green, fruitful, healthy and prosperous. What if the seed had given up because it was too pressured to sprout? What if the seed felt that the pressure of the world was too unbearable and did not try to rise above the packed earth? What if the seed conceded to the forces working against it and remained stagnant where it was originally deposited? What if it resorted to self-pity, weeping, and despair? Listen to me, it would not have become what it was destined to become.

The result is a picture of reality to the potential that lies dormant and is invisible inside each and every one of us. You must push through. The yielded seed becomes a dynasty and becomes what it was possible to be. It was created with the power. It became in spite of circumstances that appeared to be hindrances and impossibilities. Can you imagine the circumstances that surrounded the seed? There appeared to be no help and no future, for after all there was nothing evident but dirt! Nonetheless, dirt was the necessary environment; growth is impossible without it. What is your environment? You must be in the right environment with the proper mindset to prosper. Water does not boil or freeze without the proper conditions. Plants don't grow unless they are in the right environment. Seeds die lest they have a suitable place to grow.

There will always be someone or something that appears to be an obstacle to your advancement. Some people and circumstances will try to keep you from your goal. That's the way it works. Don't run! They can't stop you. They are there to bless you. They become your dirt!

Always remember your greatest obstacle and your only obstacle is you! Only you can hold you back. I encourage you not to be afraid. Let go of fear! If fear continues to abide, just do it afraid! Fear of failure, I believe, is really not as much our struggle as fear of success. JUST DO IT! Now is the time for you to yield to the universe and begin to unfold into your season. You do not have to look for wealth, or greatness, it is already inside you. YOU WERE

BORN RICH! You need only to un-tap the power and mindset the leads to WEALTH. To be continued…

Chapter 2 / Don't Be a Fool

Tonya Patterson

It was August of 1999. I was an only child of a single mom, and a single parent of my son Lamar. He was about to start 5th grade. I had been a helper in children's church for several months when the leaders asked me to start giving the message in children's church. Believing that I was not adequately prepared to serve in such a capacity, I graciously declined. I continued to serve as helper.

A few weeks later, I applied and interviewed for a volunteer prayer partner position at Trinity Broadcasting Network (TBN); praying the Lord would use me for His glory to help someone else. One night I received a call from someone crying and asking for prayer to stop worshipping Satan. He sounded very sincere, yet deathly afraid. I had never received a prayer request as specific as this before. The caller went on to say that he had been reading from a satanic bible for several weeks. Actually, I didn't even know such a bible existed, nevertheless I told him to burn it.

The next voice I heard was immensely sinister—forceful, loud, angry and gruesome. It sounded like a cross between an animal growling and a human being speaking English simultaneously, but in a very deep voice. Coming to attention in my seat, I nearly jumped out of my skin as though I had just driven over a speed bump that I had not foreseen. Will, the prayer warrior seated next to me, noticed my reaction and came onto the call with me.

By this time nothing but foul, ghoulish threats were being growled though the phone. There was no sound of the caller, who I will call Thomas. I told the growler to identify himself, and then commanded him to come out of Thomas in Jesus' Name. Will exclaimed, "Thomas, just say 'Jesus!'" In a weak far off sounding voice we heard Thomas say "Jesus' name". Then it sounded like there was a phone scuffle and the call abruptly ended. We remained in prayer for Thomas all night while the other prayer warriors accepted incoming prayer request calls.

The next day at work I received a call from my neighbor who said my house was on fire, and the fire trucks were already there. It had apparently started in a wall shared by my townhouse and that of the adjoining neighbor's townhouse. It seemed like the growler was making good on his threats.

Well, needless to say, by the time I arrived home, my son and I were homeless. The Red Cross put us in a hotel for about two weeks. I tried to enroll my son in school, but the school would not accept the hotel's address even though that was where we lived. My aunt Gwen told me that she would give me a copy of her house key and we could stay with her. Lamar could attend school around the corner. Gwen only lived five minutes from our burnt house. We thought our prayers had been answered.

Next we heard a voice message from Gwen saying she wasn't going to make the key because of pressure from my mom. My mom was saying that Lamar and I would come live with her if Gwen wasn't involving herself, so Gwen was going to stay out of it.

My son cried when we heard that message. Keep in mind my mom lived across town, far from my job and in a different school district. I did not need additional stressors.

All the apartments that we could afford had waiting lists. The cause of the fire was found to be undetermined and I discovered that my Home Owner's Insurance had lapsed. My son had now missed the first two days of school. Lamar didn't even have school clothes. It seemed like things were darker than ever.

I continued to serve, but had not said anything about our displacement to our church family. But, my pastor came to talk to me about it. Evidently, Lamar had said something in children's church when I was in adult service. Pastor Benefield prayed for us and told me about the church's food program. Miraculously, the next day, closed doors opened.

The closest apartments to my temporary job had a vacant apartment for us, and they accepted the first month's rent via a Red Cross voucher. The apartment was in walking distance to Lamar's new school and my work. I enrolled Lamar the next day with my new lease and without a utility bill, as I did not have a bill yet. I explained that we had been displaced by a fire. When I returned to pick him up, he was still sitting in the office where I had left him. My heart sank.

I couldn't believe that they had left him out of class all day. Lamar was wearing a blue t-shirt with a little black boy on it. The front read, "I know I'm special" and the back read, "Because God don't make no junk." The principal had not allowed him to attend class and even insisted on a home visit. When she arrived, she handed me a bag of food from her freezer, then viewed where we slept in sleeping bags on the floor and ate on TV trays. That's all we had—and we were thankful.

The company where I worked took up a small offering for us. We were able to repair the house minimally with a home repair grant, which was just enough to bring it to a habitable city ordinance standard. God was revealing His goodness. He made our enemies our footstools and all grace abound toward us. Hallelujah!!! Glory be to God.

I invite you to taste and see that The Lord is good. You are the apple of God's eye and He wants to withhold no good thing from you. You are special to Him. Make no mistake—Jesus loves you and He wants to be your Lord and Savior. Can you say Lord Jesus? *Lord Jesus please forgive me of all my sins. I believe that you died on the cross for my sins and that you rose again the third day.*

Right now I open the door to my heart, invite you and receive you into my heart, as my only Lord and Savior. Thank you for saving me. Amen

Results of Salvation

"not condemned"...John 3:18

"hath everlasting life"..John 3:36

"he is a new creature"..............................2 Corinthians 5:17

"the children of God"...Romans 8:6

"heirs of God"..Romans 8:7

"peace I give unto you"...John 14:27

"Spirit of God dwell in you"...............................Roman 8:9

"names are in the book of life"......................Philippians 4:3

In the Word of God

"desire.....milk of the word"..................................1 Peter 2:2

"thy word have I hid in mine heart"................Psalm 119:11

"were written for our learning"........................Romans 15:4

"scripture.....is profitable".......................2 Timothy 3:16, 17

"Study to show thyself approved"................3 Timothy 2:15

"Thy word is a lamp"…...........................Psalm 119:105

"delight is in the law of the LORD"..................Psalm 1:1, 2

The Importance of Prayer

"by prayer and supplication".......................Philippians 4:6, 7

"call upon the name of the LORD"..................Psalm 116:17

"ye shall ask"..John 15:7

"ask and it shall be given you".........................Luke 11:9, 10

"and when thou prayest................................Mathew 6:5-15

"pray without ceasing"....................1 Thessalonians 5:17, 18

"Praying always with all prayer"...................Ephesians 6:18

"Take ye heed, watch and pray"..........................Mark 13:33

In the Importance of Fellowship

"Not forsaking the assembling".....................Hebrews 10:25

"teaching…one another"………………........Colossians 3:16

"Speaking to yourselves"...............................Ephesians 5:19

"the body...hath many members"………..1 Corinthians 12:12

"members should have ...care"….......1 Corinthians 12:25-27

Chapter 3 / The Love of a Mother

Letitia Alexander

Being a mother is the one area of my life of which I am most proud. But at one point, I was going through the most bizarre transitional phase of my life—a breast cancer diagnosis. But, my daughters made it very clear that my presence was necessary, and they wanted and needed me to be around.

They shared how they admired my strength, but that it was ok to let go and cry! Little did they know I was doing a lot of that, but it was on the shoulders of Him who knew all and could heal all—my Lord and Savior Jesus Christ. I know Him to be my personal Savior and He's got me. He's got you, too. Many experience similar pain and trepidation, but at the end of the day the Lord is the one I'm choosing to believe. If He said I am healed by His stripes, then I shall be, in Jesus name.

When I received the news of my breast cancer diagnosis, I believed it was a death sentence. I lay on my sofa, sobbing over the news of my new found enemy. Having been stricken with cancer tends to take one down the road of self pity. At first, I was focused on how my life would never be the same again. In fact, I thought my life was coming to the end.

At the time, I was swimming my way out of some pretty sizable debt, so dying seemed to be the easy way out for me. I didn't have a husband and was just laid off from a teaching position. The bills were piling up. Things were so bad; I thought that if I die my children might somehow be better off without me. I had life insurance, and a last will and testament in place. Dying meant I could at least give my children more than I was able to provide, being with them. I had to learn to accept this intrusive monster that was said to be inside of me, so I made sure all my affairs were in order.

I had it all figured out except for one thing—my children were not ready for their mother to leave. In fact, it took me a while to share the news of my diagnosis of breast cancer with my daughters because I couldn't imagine what this news was going to do to them.

For me, being a mother is a highly respectable position— one which I take very seriously. Being a mother means to cultivate, motivate and educate—to improve upon, to encourage and to inspire my children. Therefore, as a parent, it is my God-given duty to raise them in such a way that will develop their strengths, all in the admonition and name of Jesus.

I've also come to realize in my experience as a parent that when you have more than one child, you love them equally yet differently. For instance, my oldest daughter, Lindsay, is a humble, caring, and frugal child with a very respectful and meek demeanor. She never caused me much stress at all and to this day, she possesses the same humble, quiet spirit. She is truly a Godsend and a very successful mother of her own three children. God knew what He was doing when He blessed me with her.

My youngest daughter, Megan, is an altogether different creature. She's very headstrong and highly opinionated, yet extremely goal oriented. Everything this child has ever set out to do, she's accomplished with great success, including her time at Spellman College. Megan was the cause of much stress in my life, but only because our personalities are so similar. We're both very dominating and controlling individuals. These are traits I am working on because they are the opposite of grace and humility.

Even though both my daughters are uniquely different I know beyond a shadow of a doubt they would do anything for me, and I would do the same for them. As God's creations, we are all here to lift up, edify, and encourage one another. We are to love unconditionally, setting aside our "almost impossible" differences. We are called to live as spiritual beings in a Christ-like manner, which requires sacrificial and unconditional love.

I remember the day I gave my life to Christ. The Lord found me thinking, *"If anything ever happened to me, what would become of my two beautiful daughters? Who would take care of them"?* It never seems there is anyone who can love a child better than her mother.

That day, I was cleaning and listening to John P. Kee's "I Surrender" in my living room. It was those questions that caused me to surrender to the will of God in my life and begin to live wholly for Him alone. He cleansed me instantly from drug abuse, sexual immorality and stealing. I was utterly free from the desire for those sins.

This new path seemed easy for me and was quite simple because God already had helpmeets in place. First, it began with picking up His Word, and then studying it, showing thyself approved. He led me to a church where I was taught the Word without compromise. The pastor did not have a problem with telling it like it is—no sugar coating whatsoever.

I went on to the school of ministry to learn more of the Lord and I must say that He grew me up quite fast. I believe the Lord originally called me when I was about 12 years old and told me who I was—it scared the living daylights out of me. My response at the time was "Not me I'm too young." He finally got my attention when I was almost 30 years old, and I've been seeking to live for Christ ever since.

When I spoke to my mom, who had also been diagnosed with breast cancer and beat it with flying colors, she thought the same would be true for me. She had a lot of hope and confidence. I just couldn't seem to share that same optimism. In my mind, I had become a disappointment to the Lord, and I thought the cancer was His way of telling me "Time's up!" With the direction my life was taking, I was fine with the death sentence.

When we carry on in a certain way, living recklessly and failing to do what we know we ought to do, it communicates that we really don't care about life. There is no other way to explain the pursuit of sin. But we are called to this:

Flee sexual immorality. Every sin that a man does is outside the body, but he who commits sexual immorality sins against his own body. (1Cor. 6:18) NKJV

Clearly the Lord was not pleased or honored by the way I was living. I was sinning against God and sinning against my own body, the temple in which He dwelt. I believe I needed to change the way I chose to live. Honestly, I don't think we should expect the Lord to meet our expectations when were so caught up in disobedience. So many are living that way without a care or concern in the world. So, I kept praying and asking the Lord to help me in my struggle with sin. But as soon as a man called, I was off fulfilling the flesh.

God began to speak to me and show me my detestable ways and the fact that I was putting that man before Him.

Has the Holy Spirit ever confronted you with the sin in your life?

The Lord had to get my attention again, even as I am now over 40 years old. I'm back on track as the Lord is divinely moving in and through my life. The transition really all began when I moved to Atlanta where I didn't have a job or a place to live. I was in the wilderness—totally dependent upon Him. The Lord was stripping me of everything I've known to bring me into a place where I was totally dependent on Him. Though I was afraid, He has blessed me with families that allowed me to stay in their homes while undergoing my cancer treatments. God had a plan for me and all I can do in the process is walk by faith and trust Him with all of my heart, mind, soul, body and strength.

With cancer, you literally become a different individual during treatment. You lose the life you once had. It seems as though everything is being stripped away from you internally, while the therapy almost literally eats you up from the inside out, zapping you of all strength and energy. Yet, as I was enduring, I also knew I must fight through it by continuing to pray and lean not to my own understanding, but keep acknowledging Him in everything I do.

The enemy has intensified and stepped up his game. But, the bottom line is this: I trust the Lord and I believe with all of my heart, mind, soul, body and strength that He has me and I know He is with me. He has not left me nor forsaken me. And, this too shall pass. I know this because the Lord is placing so many people in my life to which I am able to minister. I thank God for the opportunity to serve. This is the key: to be available to God. Allow Him to use you as He pleases and no matter what you may be going through. Know that the Lord has you and will take care of you.

Chapter 4 / The Lord is Good!

Tanya Norwood

We feed our body with food to remain healthy and we deposit money into our bank account in order to pay our bills. So, too, we must also renew our minds daily with the things of God in order to live a prosperous life. We are His. He created us and we innately know Him.

Years ago, my mind was in bondage. The hopelessness and despair I felt was so dark that I wanted to kill myself. But, I knew the Word of God. Deep within, I heard, "Tanya, I know the plans I have for you, plans to prosper you and not to harm you, plans to give you hope, a future, and an expected end."

The Lord told the Israelites to keep His commandments before them lest they forget their God, the One who brought them out of bondage. The same is true for us. We must continuously hide the Word of God in our hearts. Be not conformed to this world, but be ye transformed by the renewing of your mind, that we may prove that which is good and acceptable and perfect will of God.

God did not create me to live depressed; this is not of His Kingdom. Poverty denotes serious lack of the means for proper existence. Because I was out of relationship with Him for an extended period of time, I began to experience a seriously impoverished state of mind. But I knew the Word of God.

> *For God has not given us a spirit of fear, but of power and of love and of a sound mind. (2 Timothy 1:7) NKJV*

> *I have come that they might have life, and that they might have it more abundantly. (John 10:10) NKJV*

When we deposit money into our bank account, over time it compounds interest and nets a return. The same is true when we renew our minds. Every time I would affirm my trust in God and rely on his sufficiency, I would put a coin into His treasury. In return, I began building equity in preparation for days of trouble. The Lord keeps safely in His heart all trust invested in Him, with interest compounded continuously. The more I told God I trusted Him, the more He empowered me to move from poverty in my mind to prosperity in my thoughts.

As I learn to lay out my concerns before God, speaking candidly, pouring out my heart, talking to Him about my struggles and feelings of inadequacy, and thanking Him for the answers; the more I am able to focus on His presence and promises. As I no longer skimp on my time with God, spending quality time with Him, He prepares me for the trials and tribulations and for Kingdom building.

I've experienced firsthand that while in the midst of the storm, there is peace, and God's promises are true. God's peace is far more wonderful than the human mind can understand. His peace will keep your thoughts and your heart quiet and at rest as you trust in Christ Jesus. Oh, put God to the test and see how kind He is. See for yourself the way His mercies shower down on all who trust in Him. He can and will calm the storms that rage. God's Word assured me that He would heal my wounds and His hands would make me whole. God's desire for me is to have a sound mind.

God knows the outcome of a situation before it even arises, but He wants us to see His power and deliverance in action. He knows what He can do. He wants us to know it also. There is no need to have a poverty mentality when prosperity is available to us through the peace of God and His presence. Invite His Son Jesus into your life as Savior and learn to make Him Lord over every area of every day. Through learning and living out the Word of God, you too can have peace, His presence and a sound mind; Oh taste and see that the Lord is good!!!

Chapter 5 / Love Sought Me Out and Brought Me Out
Shawntell Sherrod

I will begin this chapter by giving glory to God. I am thankful for all that He has done in my life. I have no doubt that I did not search for Him, but that He sought me out. I am totally convinced that even before I knew who I was in Christ, and even before I surrendered my life to Him, He was near me all along.

I now understand that the devil never knew my future, but that he did recognize a person with an excellent spirit. As I look back on my life, I have no doubt that the devil was trying to kill me all along. "How do I know this", you ask? Because, I know that the devil knows what our Heavenly Father can do through a person who is teachable and totally surrendered to His will.

My heart aches with love when I think of all that my Father has done for me. I know when I read the Bible—the truths in the Bible—I know that it is truly one of the greatest expressions of love. Our Father has not only sent His Son, our Lord and Savior, to redeem us—to reconcile us to

Himself; but He then sent His Holy Spirit to live in us and work through us continuously.

The most beautiful thing to me about how our Father chooses to work is that the Holy Spirit moved upon the hearts of Jesus' Apostles to write down the new covenant. This is that beautiful written revelation of Himself—our guide for life. I think sometimes how blessed they were to walk with Christ. But, today I feel more blessed because as Jesus was the Word in the flesh, through His Spirit and by special revelation, the Word now dwells on the inside of us. That is awesome to me. We are as Christ is in this World, as we behold Him in all His Glory. My Spirit is so overjoyed.

I struggle with words sometimes when I think about it—not because I lack the words but because He has done so much for me that it is hard for me to narrow it down. I just know anything that He has planned for me and anything He allows me to go through, will all work out for the good because I love Him—and because He first loved me. Let me tell you my story.

My Life: Age 12

This was a time in my life that I was going through more things than any child should have to go through. Not that I tell this story to bash my mom, but the truth is what it is. My mom didn't hate me but she did everything in her power to make me feel like she did. I wasn't a very well-kept child. I didn't have the basic necessities. I went without food and proper clothing for most of my young life.

I'm not sure what time of the year it was, but I do know that this was the time that God revealed himself to me. It was a quiet evening and my mom was gone, and we were left home alone. My brothers and sisters had gone out playing in the neighborhood; of course we had been told not to go anywhere. I was pretty much the only one that listened—well, most of the time.

We were left with no food and no electricity; and at that time, we didn't even have water. It was at this time when the urge to read the Bible came to me, and I was led to a Bible which I'm sure belonged to my grandmother. The Scripture I immediately came to was Psalms 27:10.

When my father and my mother forsake me, then the LORD will take me up.

Coincidence? With God, there are no coincidences. In my heart at that moment, I felt the warmth and love of God, and I was caused to yearn for more of that feeling. I sought out more of His Words because in me was created a hunger and thirst for God's Word that would continually need to be nurtured. About a week later, I confessed Jesus as my Lord and Savior and received my eternal salvation.

My Life: Age 16

This was a time when I had been put out in the street for absolutely no reason. It was cold and I spent most of my time just walking and wandering around. I can remember around this time that I had gone almost two weeks without food. But, what I remember most now is how I never got sick, even when I slept in vacant houses as the outdoor temperatures often plunged below zero.

I can recall a couple of young guys in the neighborhood we grew up with. One day, my twin sister was out there with me and she was also very hungry. They asked us if we needed food because they had an idea of what was going on. We told them we hadn't eaten in a while so they brought us food. Despite the fact that they stole it from a nearby store, I will never forget what they did because of the risk and sacrifice involved.

Oh, what I would give to have been able to see all the invisible spiritual things that were going on around me because I know that it had to be a battle. One day I had walked so long that when nightfall came, I took a seat on a park bench just to take a rest. I know that I had to be exhausted because what seemed to be just a couple of hours was much more. I was awakened by the sun coming up. This wasn't a safe place to sleep unguarded, so I know I was protected by angels.

My Life: Age 18

My boyfriend and I had come together at an early age, yet he was four years older. During the course of our relationship, we had a child together, our son Anthony. We were going through so much because our families were not supportive of us having a baby.

But one day we were coming back from one of the many court visits, I suppose that my natural soul had enough. As we were waiting on the bus, in the middle of the road I cried out to God in anger and frustration. I said to Him, "God where are you? You called me to believe in you but you're never here! Why are you allowing this? Where are you when I need you?"

After this very public and tearful meltdown, my son's father and I got on the bus—my eyes red from crying—and we began our trip home. Keep in mind—we took this trip frequently past the same bridges and the same overpasses every time. So, as we went back, I noticed large writing on one of the overpasses that I know wasn't there when we headed downtown.

It said, "Trust Jesus." I looked over at it and I paused. I looked at my son's father and asked him if he saw it—he did not. Then we passed another bridge and there were large letters which said "He will never leave you." Then I looked at my son's father and the people on the bus to see if anyone was looking in the direction I was looking. No one was. So after about 2 to 3 more minutes, I saw another bridge and the words that were posted were, "He will never let you down."

So, at this point I was feeling a little puzzled and unsure of how to feel. We came to a stop, and a person who I thought was a man got on the bus. I will never forget how he looked—he was a tall black man wearing a khaki colored trench coat. He sat right at the front of the bus by the door. When the bus proceeded to move, the man began to sing. He sang with the most beautiful voice quite loudly and I just stared at him. I was mesmerized by his voice and then the natural senses started to kick in. I noticed that no one else was looking at him but me—not even my son's father.

Now I have to tell you that if someone gets on a bus and begins to say anything loudly, people are going to take notice. Yet, no one but me seemed to even manage a glance. The song that he was singing was unknown to me, but the chorus of the song went like this: "Everything is going to be all right when Jesus comes." So as I listened to him, I became filled with warmth and comfort and joy, and then there was a peace that came over me—a peace that hasn't left me to this day. This man—perhaps an angel who took the form of a man—sang this song all the way to my next stop.

This is a day I will never forget. It is just one of many ways that my Lord and Savior has revealed to me that He would never leave me nor forsake me. There is truly none like Him!

My Life: Age 19-23

This is a time in any young person's life when they should thrive and find their way. But, I came up with the "bright idea" to earn a living by working at a strip club.

Yeah, I said "strip club". I bet you didn't see that coming! But, we know that the law condemns the best of us but grace saves the worst of us; Glory to God for His Grace. Never let anyone tell you that you are unfit to be used by God because of anything that you have done in your past.

Though I only worked at the club for about four weeks, I feel compelled to tell this part of my story because it is such a beautiful testimony of how God loved and pursued me. While working at this club, I immediately started to see how differently I was treated in comparison to the other girls. Because I was in Oklahoma, the laws limited the degree of nudity in these clubs. So, I was never fully nude, though the clothes were very scandalous and I did go topless. Most of my money I made was while sitting and talking to the men who frequented the business. I know people would think that isn't true but it was for me. I choose to believe that the Lord was protecting me from what I had gotten myself into. Yes, He was shielding my heart right in the midst of this mess!

Nearly every guy I sat in front of asked me why I was there. They said that I didn't belong there and that I didn't fit in. That was confusing, considering they were there to see girls. Within a couple of weeks, another man said the same thing to me. Commenting on my beauty, he just felt I deserved better and he said so. We talked for a few hours about why I was there and what I was seeking, all the while he was giving me money because he knew I needed it. Then, suddenly he told me that he was going to come back in the following week and that he was going to give me a large sum of money so that I didn't need to work in those places again. I believed him for some reason. Sure enough, he returned and I left the industry. So who thinks that wasn't my God, my Lord?

But how many of you know that it's not that simple? I can assure you that while the Lord was working, the devil was definitely at work as well. I left as I promised because he kept his word. But, I had met another man there who was 19 years older than me and was into some things that I was naive about at the time. He was a handsome older man who seemed much younger. He gave me everything, which was his means of seduction. I traveled with him, he took me out to dinner, and he bought me a lot of nice things.

Remember that I never even had basic necessities as I was growing up, so to suddenly have access to the necessities and more was very exciting. As a couple of years passed, he continued to treat me well, but things were about to dramatically change. He was dealing drugs and involved in other illegal activities. He knew I would not approve and he tried to change his ways. This was a man who had been a corporate executive but greed caused him to stray.

His attempts to live in decent, honest ways weren't working out for him. He lashed out at me one day simply because I asked him a question. He began to hit me and broke my jawbone. I felt the bones crack and they were rubbing together, and I couldn't speak. He didn't take me to the hospital nor would he let anyone near me. After about two weeks, I still wasn't talking very well but the bones begin to heal.

The utilities were shut off and it was very cold. I can remember being in the back room by the fireplace, huddled on the floor on a mat trying to keep warm. I believe that hypothermia set in, and I have no doubt that I died. I can remember lying on the floor with a blanket pulled over my head—and I saw a horse. I was 100% sure of this as the horse seemed to be pulling the blanket from over my head. It was nudging me and I opened my eyes. I could see a bright light but then realized there was no one there but me. So, I fought my sleep until eventually he had arrived back with some more wood for the fire.

There wasn't much more I could take. This is when I decided to leave, and he wrapped a phone cord around my throat. I passed out and when I regained consciousness, I had a hemorrhage in my eye. So I had no choice but to leave.

My Life: Age 28

By this point I was thinking a lot different about who I am in Christ. It wasn't anywhere near the understanding I have now, but I knew there was more than what I had seen and experienced in life and in love.

By this point, I had been taking care of my little sister. She had graduated high school and then left to go to Texas with her dad. I decided that I wanted to enroll in college. Keep in mind, I only had a seventh grade education. So, I went into the college campus and decided I wanted to become a court reporter. After I finishing speaking with a college counselor and taking a tour, she asked me for my diploma. I told her I did not have a high school diploma. She told me that I could not enroll without one. So, I boldly looked her in the eye and said that I would be back.
.

I left there that day and contacted various places to get a GED or take a course to test out of high school. Meanwhile, the guy whom I was leaving was making all kind of comments about how I couldn't do it, I wouldn't succeed. But, by then there had been a fire kindled in me that inspired me to push forward, no matter what others might say.

I walked back into the college and I can assure you she was surprised to see me return. She obviously didn't think I would do it. I stopped and pulled my diploma out and showed her. She smiled.

I went on, achieving honors every semester, and graduating with a 3.47 GPA. Keep in mind, this was done while working multiple jobs, raising my son alone, and going to school full-time. I dare not rob God of His Glory. When I think of how I was almost able to memorize whole paragraphs simply by closing my eyes, I knew it has always been Him. I also know it will always be He who keeps me. It will always be He who leads; and it will always be He who gives me the ability. It will always be He who teaches me to prosper; and it will always be He who loves me like none other. It will always be He who defends my honor and upholds my best interest. Amazing love!

As if that wasn't blessing enough—my Lord and Savior then gave me 2 inventions and a corporation, which I am in the process of organizing. He has given me 12 books to write and I have no doubt that I will write every one of them. He has given me a website with a commission to edify women and minister the Word. Even in all this, I know that all of these things He has given me are just the beginning.

I want you to know that any Word that you hear from the Lord cannot be taken from you. You would have to abort that vision. So, I am here to encourage you to hold on to God's unchanging hand because our Father is in the business of seeking out and bringing out! So come out of Lo-debar, and walk into the land flowing with milk and honey.

I know that God is my only source, so it is all being done without compromise, anxiety or fear. My Father is not a deadbeat dad and if He said it, it is done already. So, I walk it out in faith. I want you to do the same because He is faithful!

Christmas 2011

Like so many Christmases before, I was alone on Christmas, in 2011. However this Christmas proved to be very different. Though I was there without anyone in the natural, I knew I wasn't there alone. It wasn't like the Christmases in the past where I was crying myself to sleep. What made the difference this particular Christmas is that I knew I wasn't alone.

This testimony is so dear to me because of the personal time that I shared with my Father that day. I felt His presence the moment He entered the room. There is no mistaking His presence or His voice.

I struggle with the words to express how special He made me feel this day. He went out of His way to let me know that He loved me. I heard him repeatedly state to me, "I love you." The first time I smiled because I heard Him loud and clear. Then, just about 10 minutes later, I was rejoicing in him and worshipping him in song and I stopped for a while. Then, I began painting my nails and making melody in my heart. It was then when I heard Him say again, "I love you."

I can tell you it wasn't just that He said it—it was how He said it. He said it with such intensity and such tenderness, and He made it personal. Yes, He loves us all; but this day at this moment, He wanted me to know that He loves me and not to minimize how much he loves me individually.

His voice is intoxicating and yet reviving. It simply moves through you, filling you and touching every part of your spirit and soul. I can honestly say that I began to blush like a two-year-old child. I literally giggled and blurted out, "Oh God", as I laughed. I began to blush like a two-year-old child and called Him daddy. I said Abba.

I never had a dad, but My Father—the Heavenly Father filled me with His love and cradled His daughter. He let me know that I am a cherished and beloved jewel. So, I need no validation from anyone but Him, and that has already been done through the Blood of Jesus! I am the Apple of God's eye! So are you…so rest in His arms and in His love. He's got you!

For those who aren't familiar with my testimony about the many languages that he gave me in the gift of tongues, read my first book "Woman Submit, Under Man's Mission Not Under His Foot."

This day we had beautiful intimate time together in conversation in a language unknown to me but very fluent to my Spirit, and in silence He made His presence known. I can say it was one of the most beautiful Christmases that I have ever had in my life. I say this because I know I literally spent it with my Father in my Spirit. I know that I was there in the heavenly place with Him enjoying that day.

Note of Encouragement

So, brothers and sisters, once you have conceived a thing in your heart, don't let anyone or anything rob you of it—not even your own feelings of inadequacy. Neither let your contradictory speaking cause your spirit to abort the thing and promise it has conceived. We are the children of the Most-High God and we shall have whatever we say! So guard your heart and mouth, and move away from negative people.

I give God the glory and the praise that is due to Him, for I know he preserves me. He lovingly and tenderly guides me and instructs me without condemning me; and when I need more grace, He gives more. He is an unlimited and fully sufficient supply! He is my Lord and Savior, my Father, and the Most High. Know that nothing you can do will ever disqualify you because Christ paid a price once for all. You will qualify because of His blood.

Remember that we live Holy because we were made righteous; we don't live holy trying to become righteous. That has been done already.

So, in the name of Jesus, walk out of the realm of failure, fear, darkness and confusion; and enter the arena of success. Everything in the Kingdom operates by faith, so in faith note that our heavenly Father has made you fit.
But, sometimes we have to take some things off to put some things on. Remove the garments of your old former self, and put on the garment of Righteousness with which our Lord and Savior has clothed you. Wear it without shame and know that you are—we are—the seed that the Lord has blessed. We are the Lord's, so by the Spirit we judge all things, yet we are judged of no one!

Brothers and sisters, understand that we are a new creation in Christ and that we have been grafted into the Messiah. Behold, the fresh and new has come. So, forever say goodbye to whom you used to be. Put on your new nature for you/we are crucified with Christ, nevertheless we live, yet not you/we but it is Christ lives in us.

I want you to take from this the fact that anything that you can imagine, and anything that you can conceive from the word of God in your heart can be brought forth into the natural. This is a powerful thing. What this should tell you is just as Jesus said, that if we have faith as the grain of mustard seed and we say to a mountain be thou removed and cast into the sea, this should be done and that nothing shall be impossible to those who believe.

It is all about faith, and our understanding that as we behold Christ just as He is in all His love, all His greatness, all His sufficiency, and all His power—as we truly look upon Him, we are transformed into that very image from one degree of glory to another.

I just want to magnify God and give thanks to my Father. I want to give glory to God for all He has done and for all that I know He is doing. I want to thank Him for what He did for me, for all of us, simply for the beauty that was set before Him. He became sin and took everything that we deserved. He died for us and has been given full reign and authority over him who once had the power over death. I thank God for that day on the Cross that Christ not only paid the price for our sins, but he forever made us righteous. He nailed the Law to the Cross, the ordinances that were written to reveal man's need for a Savior.

Thy Kingdom come, Thy will be done in Earth as it is in Heaven! Now thanks be unto God who always causes us to triumph in Christ!

Chapter 6 / To Be Continued...

Dr. Inetta J Cooper

She came home from school and opened the door to her lunch, which consisted of homemade biscuits, syrup and a glass of milk. She removed her school clothes and put on her work clothes, and then ate her lunch. As she left the house, her dog followed her down the long dirt road, across the main highway to the fields where others were picking cotton.

She grabbed her sack, putting it around her neck, and then started picking at the end of the row. As she picked, her dog anticipated her next move by finding his spot every few feet to relax under the shade of the cotton bush. Her tiny fingers pulled the cotton out of its snug little home, and she placed it in her sack, continuing this ritual until the bush was desecrated of all the cotton. Then she moved down the row to the next one. Not much was on her mind, just how the day went at school, the math assignment that she had trouble with and the difficult teacher, Ms. Smith. "Why does she hate me?" she thought. But then, she hated all the kids whose parents weren't teachers or who had factory jobs; or if the kids were dark skinned. Anyhow, she shrugged it off and concentrated on how fast she could reach her dog down the cotton row.

Finally, it was too dark to pick anymore and they left the field to go home. She thought about homework but then her mother started yelling about getting pails of water so she could cook supper. So, she took the pails and went outside to the pump to get water. She struggled with the heavy pail of water, taking it to the kitchen. Then, she picked up the other pail and went back out to the pump for another. This pail was heavier than the first one, but she made it. She lifted it up on the table, with trembling arms. Then, she went to her room that also doubled as the family room, and tried to start her homework. She was so tired; she fell asleep on top of the book. She woke up to more yelling about supper being ready. She ate in silence, watching who she thought was her mother and father. But, it would soon be revealed that they were not.

She sat on the back steps rubbing the head of her grateful dog and thankful for his unconditional love. She was so excited that her cousins invited her to a cookout at their pastor's house. This was the first time she had hot dogs on a grill! They tasted so good! She had fun riding in the car with her cousins, all around her age. She felt really happy. She ran into the house when they dropped her off, with excitement, having had so much fun. She began to tell her Mom and Dad about the great time she had.

Then her mother calmly told her she stayed out too long. "What do you mean?" she asked. "I was with my cousins, they were driving and I came home with them." Her mother sternly said, "You are late coming home, and you must be whipped." She began to cry "NO! I WAS RIDING WITH MY COUSINS, YOU SAID I COULD GO!" Her mother grabbed a belt and lunged at her, while her father sat quietly, saying not a word. She ran out the back door and her mother ran after her. She made it to the railroad tracks before her mother grabbed her by the hair, pulling her back to the house, where she mercilessly whipped welts all over her body. She didn't understand—this was wrong! Why didn't she want me to enjoy time with children my own age, and we were at the Pastor's house, for God sakes! This was just wrong!

In years to come, she would be beaten many more times by her mother. But, it was her piano lessons that literally saved her life. She could escape in her music from all the troubles she would face in years to come. Her father would continue to sit in silence, while she screamed in pain…from the physical abuse and from the lack of love. She would find out later that her mother was really not her mother, and her father was really not her father. She would grow up, get married, be a battered wife, have children, have much success in her career, start a worldwide ministry, start a successful business, write a book, send two sons to college, and……

Well, I'm still under construction, I'm still on the Potter's Wheel, and I'm still being processed. There are many more goals in life I'd like to accomplish, and many more strives I'd like to make in God. Philippians 1:6 talks about every good work that is begun in you shall be completed. Undeniably, I stand on the promise of God that no matter what I've gone through, no matter what I will go through, My God will empower me to complete His work, according to His will.

Yes, I'm still pressing, still wanting, and still seeking God's will for my life. I'm trying to use every situation and every circumstance to build me up to the next level. When life threw me in a hole and put dirt on me, I packed it under my feet and climbed out. I'm still climbing. God sheltered me during the storms. He hid me under His wings, and if He did that for me, He will do it for anyone. We have to stay in His Word, and keep it on our heart and in our mouth. It will keep us when we don't want to be kept, or when we don't deserve to be kept. He loves us so much and would never leave us, and never forsake us. No, it's not over yet, not until God says it over, and for me God says….TO BE CONTINUED.

Chapter 7 / Transforming Grace
Carmelo Colon, Jr.

Daniel 4:2 "I thought it good to declare the signs and wonders that the Most High God has worked for me." NKJV

I came to Philadelphia at the age of seven, from Puerto Rico; our family lived there for around 20 years. After high school, I pursued a career in cosmetology.

As a young man I began to engage the club scene in Philadelphia. When you're young you like to party, but I was a raised in church and this crazy partying life took a toll in me. During this crazy time, I met a girl who also attended the same school, and was traveling the same career route. We began to date and one day I moved from my parents' house to live with her. Soon after getting married in 1985, she became pregnant with our son, Ryan David Colon.

After the birth of our son, we soon returned to the partying life. Drinking and drug use caused everything in our marriage to move backwards instead of forward. We were confused because we had been without solid direction. When I saw my life heading in the path of destruction, I knew things were not right.

One day I went out to have a few drinks. I had recently purchased a new car and decided to drive to Philadelphia to show my parents—I never made it. I was in a major accident where the car flipped three times and I lost track of my surroundings. When I eventually opened my eyes, I found myself in the hospital with internal bleeding. My face was seriously injured and I was bruised from head to toe.

Because of the circumstances, I was charged with driving under the influence. When I found myself in a cell at Eagleville, to my surprise, there was a Bible. I immediately thought the Lord must have something specific planned for my life because I could have died in that car accident. Later when I was able to see the totaled remains of my car, I was so shocked I passed out. It was unbelievable to me that anyone could have survived that crash—and in this case, *anyone* was me. As a result, I believed the Lord had a purpose for my life. But, it didn't take long before I began to spiral downward again, doing the same self-destructive things over and over.

Even though I got clean from alcohol and drug use, my wife informed me that she wanted a divorce. Though I accepted this, the divorce hurt me very much because I loved my wife. After she left me, my life seemed very empty. Not knowing where to turn during this time, I chose the world of drugs, alcohol and the reckless partying life instead of the Lord. I wasn't really happy.

The partying continued with another friend who was also a hairdresser. This is how I would eventually become involved in the gay lifestyle. Every week, I went to gay clubs and began dating men—but I wasn't happy. That kind of life took a toll on me. I felt immoral, dirty, and not right in the eyes of God. It was then that I asked the Lord to please take this way of life away from me. "This is not my lifestyle—this is not how I want to live."

I kept asking the Lord to please reform my life. Change me. I fervently prayed and asked the Lord to cleanse me from this sin, this burden that I am carrying, and this wickedness that has become a spiritual stronghold. I wanted it out in the name of Jesus.

The next day after this humbling prayer to the Lord, I met a couple from church who extended an invitation for me to attend church with them. The services provide an altar call where I could go before the Lord with all my needs. I was falling in love with this church and eventually I did go to the altar where the leaders prayed for me. I had already asked the Lord to do what I needed for Him to do in my life. I needed liberation from this sin because I believed I was not born a homosexual.

The pastor of Sion church, Rev. Paul Leduc, prayed for me. I fell back and was on the floor near the altar. I do not know how long I was there but when I got up, I felt very different. I was talking different. I was walking different. I said to my Father God, "Why do I feel different? Only you know how I feel because you made me feel this way."

I continued attending church for almost 15 years. The Lord delivered me from the wickedness of alcohol, drugs, and homosexuality. I was being transformed. It was then that I started attending the Bible Institute where I studied for four years. Rain, sunshine, cold weather or hot weather—it didn't matter; I was there with perfect attendance and achieving the honor roll. I graduated after 4 years but then I slipped and went back to my old ways.

I thought no one in church loved me. People looked at me differently. The only one who looked at me with love was "Jesus" because He knows who I am. Yet, I turned my back to the Lord and went back to the world. I knew He loved me, but I was so confused.

One day I declared this was not for me and begged for forgiveness. God says a person can fall 7 times and He will lift him up. After much prayer, the Lord delivered me from all my sins again. I thank God my Father for delivering me from all my sins. I'm cleansed by His blood thru the work of the Holy Spirit. I thank God for everything He has done in my life. I am nobody. The Bible says:

"Therefore, if anyone is in Christ, he is a new creation; old things have passed away; behold, all things have become new." (2 Corinthians 5:17) NKJV

I am a new creature in Christ!!

This is my testimony. I will forever be thankful to the Lord for loving me and transforming my life.

ALLELLUYIA!

Chapter 8 / Pursuing Joy & Prosperity

Brother Peter Edwin

The title of this book is derived from the scripture. Any man who believes and walks according to God's precepts and promises truly lives a successful and prosperous life.

> *The blessing of God makes one rich, and He adds no sorrow with it. (Prov 10:22)*

I am not talking about the kind of riches or wealth gained through worldly ways, the way the world views achieving success—I mean the blessing of God which makes an individual rich with no sorrow or struggles attached to it. As a blessed person, whether man or woman, there are things that should be present in your life—joy and satisfaction, peace of mind, happiness, contentment, improved health and flow of energy, all of which are evidences of blessing from God.

When I say life full of joy and energy, I mean the very one David the Psalmist talked about in the scriptures.

> *You will show me the path of life; in your presence is fullness of joy; at your right hand are pleasures forevermore.* (Psalm 16:11) NKJV

David knows quite well that he serves a living God who answers prayer. For this reason, he seeks to always be joyful despite his circumstances. He does not waver or shake but goes to the presence of God
because he knows that only God can break the back of his enemies or solve his problems. He trusts God.

> *I lay down and sleep, I awoke, for the Lord sustained me, I will not be afraid of ten thousands of people who have set themselves against me all around... (Psalm 3:5-6) NKJV*
> *I will both lie down in peace and sleep; for you alone O Lord, make me dwell in safety. (Psalm 4:8) NKJV*

This signifies how confident, safe and peaceful David feels in God's hand. God's trustworthiness and reliability give David a total assurance that no negative power can pull him down.

Similarly, we the believers are expected to do the same. Be joyful and content because we should be aware that our Redeemer lives and He will neither leave us nor forsake us. This is a joy which surpasses all human understanding.

The blessed people of the Lord experience his peace and energy and are to be full of stamina because the source of riches and prosperity is God. He lacks nothing and gives everything. Man is to make a full estimate of his ability and remind himself that the Lord is with him and absolutely nothing can defeat him. He is to remember, "I can do all things through Christ who strengthens me."

What so many individuals don't understand is that the peace you and I enjoy generates power or strength to our physical body. It contributes to our spiritual and mental reasoning. The happiness we enjoy comes directly from the Lord, an endowment and blessing from the Almighty. The joy or happiness money or property provides is temporary, but the joy of every believer is controlled by the standard of our faith in God. He will never forsake us nor leave us, no matter what circumstances.

Scripture confirms it.

These things I have spoken to you, that in Me (Jesus Christ) you may have peace. (John 16:33) NKJV

How do you feel when you study your Bible and meditate on the word of God before you go to sleep? I always sleep like a little child in a deep, restful slumber. I always sleep through the night simply because of the peace and the favor of the Almighty God. We have heard it said over and over—seek peace and let it be established in you and in your environment. Set your mind on the things of the spirit, not on trouble in the world. Let your soul be established in righteousness, peace and joy. Do you want peace? Then you need to seek peace.

So many individuals seek help where there is no help, looking for peace of mind through alcohol, drugs or other hopeless places. They need to acknowledge the presence of God and lay back, relax and enjoy the peace that only Christ Jesus has offered to them. This comes by looking into the Scripture, meditating in the words of God, claiming His promises and being obedient to His Word. Instead, they immerse themselves in a life of merely temporary wealth, in search of peace while true peace stands in their doorpost waiting for them.

Some folks develop high blood pressure, not because of the trouble or circumstances they face, but because they are allowing the trouble to give them sleepless nights. Instead, they should run to God who controls and heals both named and un-named diseases.

One thing is sure, when you accept Jesus Christ as your personal Lord and Savior, what you are saying is; "I need my sins forgiven". When Jesus Christ forgives your sins, freedom and liberty, peace, good health and deliverance come with salvation. Baptism in the name of the Father, Son and Holy Spirit confirms your new birth in Christ Jesus, your total commitment to know the truth and your willingness to grow.

The book of Psalms provides an analysis of how a prosperous or blessed man spends his life, what he does that brings glory to God and the success that should follow.

> *Blessed is the man who walks not in the counsel of the ungodly, nor stands in the paths of sinners, nor sits in the seat of the scornful; But his delight is in the law of the Lord and in his law, he meditates day and night. He shall be like a tree planted by the*

rivers of water, that brings forth his fruit in its season, whose leafs shall not wither, and whatever he does shall prosper. (Psalm 1:1-4) NKJV

Does it seem like you are among the blessed? Being blessed doesn't mean that you must have fleets of cars, houses or other extravagances. One thing you must have that is indicative of prosperity is peace and joy.

I know and am fully aware that there has been a time in life when you've probably asked God, "Are you really on my side?" Please don't ever in your mind think that it is unusual to ask yourself such question. When circumstances or storms want to engulf you or when problems are overwhelming, it's a question we all ask at one point or another.

Sometimes doubt overpowers faith and you wonder why prayers go unanswered. We fail to ask ourselves, "Are we really praying according to the will of God Almighty concerning our lives?"

Psalm 91 shares the promise to those who love God dearly. It begins with the confirmations of security with every individual who dwells in the secret place of the Almighty God. They shall abide under the shadow of the Almighty. It continues to describe how we take refuge in Him if we trust Him, and about how God will deliver every man or woman who has faith in Him. He shields us under His feathers to protect us from both seen and unseen dangers.

He then instructs us to not be afraid of the terror by night and the arrow by day, even the diseases that fly in the darkness because His eyes are set upon us. No destruction can ever pass Him to us because everything in Heaven and on Earth bows before His throne.

Knowing God means understanding Him and His ability and power—what He is capable of doing and how He operates. Our behavior changes when we understand who God the Father is. There is nothing we can do but totally rely on Him through faith—though we do not see Him, He is with us always.

As we continue walking by faith, the next formula that we need to apply is called the "power in the Word of God". In every circumstance, I seek out the Lord in scripture to understand what He wants me to know and do. I meditate on passages that apply to my situation and it seems in no time, I have clarity on the situation.

One of the most powerful messages in scripture can be found in Romans.

> *If God be for us, who can be against us?* (Romans 8:31)

Meditating on this passage allows me to see my faith overcoming the fear that the enemy had previously attacked me with.

You and I need to utilize the powerful and supernatural formula that our God has given to us right from the beginning of creation. Why did God tell us that *the power of death and life is in the tongue?* - or - *out of the mouth of babes and nursing infants you have ordained strength*? The Bible is given to us as a life manual, with directions to operate in this life provided through the Holy Spirit.

How do you feel when you forget your compass or GPS when you are travelling to a place you don't know too well? Don't you feel lost? That's exactly how you and I should feel when we refuse to use the Bible, which is life's GPS or compass.

What every believer should be careful of is that there are some behaviors that attract curses from God. Sin is a reproach and is the activity of indulging in things that have already been cursed. Sins such as jealousy, malice, greed or anger may seem like little sins, but they play a big role when present in our lives. They hinder God from pouring blessings out on our lives. We need to know the God we worship. He pays everyone according to his or her deeds. He is impartial, a mighty God in battle, and a forever living God.

Can we just be consistent and obedient to God's word and promises? Is it possible to pray and expect the best from God, and no longer entertain fear and sin? Back it up with faith. After all, you will see what the Lord will do for you.

The scripture confirms the ability of our God in the book of 1 Samuel 2:6-9.

> *The Lord kills and makes alive. He brings down to the grave and brings up. The Lord makes poor and*

makes rich. He brings low and lifts up. He raises the poor from the dust and lifts the beggar from the ash heap and sets them among the princes and makes them inherit the throne of glory! For the pillars of the earth are the Lords. He has set the world upon them, He will guard the feet of His saints.

Our God is able to do all this marvelous work that the scripture has written! Is this description of whom God is not enough for you to begin to cast your trust upon Him, to really believe in every one of His words? So many don't want to go into business or back to school because they are afraid of failure. Do you doubt the power in the word of God?

Psalm 75:6-7 confirms that our God has what it takes for us to be the best in life,

For exaltation comes neither from the east, nor from the west nor from the south. But God is the Judge; He puts down one and exalts another. NKJV

Romans 8:32 confirms God's ability to render justice and fairness to those who are obedient to His Word and to fulfill His promises to each of them. He who did not spare His own son, but delivered Him up for us all, how shall He not with Him also freely give us all things?

This question is for you to answer for yourself; no one can answer it for another. If you say that you believe God, you should equally trust and have confidence in His word without wavering. Can you sometimes take inventory of your life instead of blaming God for not answering your prayers? I do sometimes ask myself if there is something I am not doing right or if I am falling short. There is nothing wrong for someone to take an incisive look into his or her life!

Often when I study the Bible, I get excited about the meaning of so many passages. In the Gospel of Matthew, Jesus confronted His disciples on the issue of unbelief. He spoke,

> ...*if you have faith as a mustard seed, you will say to this mountain, 'Move from here to there,' and it will move...* (Matthew 17:20) NKJV

He continued to let them know that nothing will be impossible for them.

Are you are in a situation in which you think that there is no solution, or are you feeling abandoned or that God has forsaken you? I have a question for you! Do you have faith as small as a mustard seed? Can you excise or change your mental attitude a little bit, focusing on God's own ability rather than doing it on your own? Can you persevere and place your reliance on the word of God, speaking His words over and over on your problem? Sometimes it may seem that it does not work, but continue speaking and at the same time begin to visualize your anticipated result.

What is it that you believe God for? You need to stop doubting in your mind and believe His Word. You need to form the habit of repeating His promises concerning the circumstances you are facing. You need to recondition your condition because you have the ability. Ask for a specific thing, stand firmly and believe you will receive what you ask for without doubting in your heart, and you will have it. This is a proven formula prescribed by the most wonderful life manual from the Almighty God Himself.

In December of 2005, I was in a situation which no one on earth could have saved me—only God. I was shot in the face at a close range but I called the name of God Almighty and He saved my life. The doctor who took care of me is still in doubt to this day about the power of God in spite of the fact that I'm still alive. That's the kind of Father we have—if you only believe and obey Him.

Be Sure What You Are Asking God For

Ten years ago I came to the United States. When I arrived, I made a list of the things I wanted God to do for me. Out of the ten things I wrote down in my prayer list, only a few remain not yet done.

> *Then the Lord answered me and said, "Write the vision, and make it plain on the tablets that he may run who reads it for the vision is yet for an appointed time, but at the end it will speak, and it will not lie. Though it tarries, wait for it because it will surely come, it will not tarry.* (Habakkuk 2:2-4)

Some believers think God is a magician. He is not. He is the Creator of the universe. He owns everything in Heaven and on Earth. He doesn't give to you and me because we ask. He gives to us because we need it. Understand that He knows the end from the beginning and He even knows how you wish to utilize whatever He gives to you before it is provided.

The scriptures asked this question, *who is it that wants to build a house and he doesn't first calculate what the house will cost?* Everything in life is a journey and you must begin somewhere. It is said that a journey of one thousand miles begins with a single step. In the same way, if you and I need something from our God, it must be a process, He is not a magician.

I recall the day I learned the scripture, *I can do all things through Christ which strengthens me.* Since this very day, I have been operating in another level. What the Lord is telling me is that all my blessing demands obedience to God's Word. Remember God does not change according to Malachi 3:6. If He blessed the people of old—Abraham, David, Solomon, Joseph and others who walked according to His precept—He will still bless me. But, what I need to do is to renew myself to God's call to holy living and always being thankful, generous, forgiving, and above all else, remaining faithful.

Chapter 9 / Knowing your Purpose

J.B. Tremont

The Poverty

I am from the Bronx, but I never wanted my origins to define who I am. I was not ashamed of being from the Bronx, neither was I proud of it. I just did not want its past reputation to dictate my future, to define me.

Growing up, I didn't know I was poor until one day my mother enlightened me: "Girl, don't you know we are just one paycheck away from being poor," she said as she shook her head. I must have been 9 or 10 years old at the time. In my estimation, we didn't "seem" to be poor. I lived with both my mother and father—they were married, they were young, and they were employed. We lived in a clean apartment building and we never felt hunger. My mother took my sister and me clothes shopping at Macy's twice a year: in the spring for our spring and summer clothes, and in the fall for our school and winter clothes. We received great presents at Christmas; my father took us to see the new Disney movies when they were released. My parents provided the best life they could. I had no idea what it meant to be poor because they managed to provide for all of our needs.

I remember visiting my classmates' homes, but never thought twice about what they had because I was content. Even though these classmates were Caucasian, they didn't appear to have more than we had… they just lived in better neighborhoods. In fact, in some cases, we may have actually had more.

My mother's statement about our economic status changed my perspective. Although imperceptible, it caused me to start valuing wealth differently, and it began to shape my life and career decisions early. **I DID NOT WANT TO BE POOR!** I distinctly remember asking both my mother and grandmother one day, "Who makes more money, a teacher or a lawyer?" They both confirmed, "A lawyer, of course."

Although I loved to teach—I had tutored older cousins in math, and taught my younger sister how to read—I was determined right then and there that I would become an attorney because I would not be poor. This determination became a driving force in my life.

You see, God had given me the aptitude to be anything in life I set my mind to be. When I decided I would become a lawyer, I became more determined and motivated to press through the years of education to reach my goal. I held on to that plan of becoming an attorney up until my first year of law school. It was then I realized…I actually hated the study of law. I was miserable, and absolutely and utterly unhappy.

I remember calling my mother in February, during my second semester of my first year of law school, weeping and confessing, "Mom, I don't want to do this anymore! I do not like law school!" My mother begged me, "Please just complete the year. If you finish your first year and decide to stop, then I'll support your decision. But, if you ever choose to go back to law school, you will not have to repeat your first year." Both my mother's pleas and the reasonableness of her advice persuaded me not to quit at that time. Although I suffered through the completion of my first year, (nothing but the grace of God), at its end, I made the decision to stop.

During the summer following the first year, I interned with the Equal Employment Opportunity Commission (EEOC).

Midway through the internship, I knocked on my supervisor's door and humbly asked, "How did you *know* you wanted to be an attorney?" She must have sensed my confusion and sadness, so she answered my question quite candidly—but with compassion. "If I had to do it again, I would have become a journalist. But life's responsibilities and student loan repayments keep me bound to my commitment to be an attorney. Hence, if you are unsure that this is what you want to do, then DON'T DO IT!" I felt her unhappiness, yet I was relieved. Someone else truly understood what I was feeling.

It was at this time I decided I would not return to law school. I took a leave of absence; the Lord gave me a job right away and for the first time in many months, I was happy and unburdened. I felt free. I wish I could say that I never went back, but family pressure caused me to rethink my decision, "You are the first person in the family to become a lawyer." I was twenty-three years old and I caved under the pressure. I returned to law school one year later, as an evening student. During the day, I worked to pay my bills, purchased my first car and at the age of twenty-four, I purchased a home. I was very independent, graduated with a J.D. (Jurist Doctorate), and became pregnant right after I finished law school.

Have you ever heard of the expression, "One bad decision leads to another"? I was trying to make something out of my existence—but without God. I believed I could control my destiny and accomplish anything and everything on my own. Like a fool, I did not give God the glory, so I should not have been surprised when God began to take things back, that I might become aligned for "His" purpose, His will, and plan for me. You see, God's purpose for my life was not MY purpose for my life. In fact, I had no clue as to what God's purpose was for me.

I remember speaking to myself as a teenager when things were really tough, "There must be a purpose for my life. I am not dead. I am not crazy. I'm still here. Why haven't I taken myself out of here – there has to be a purpose for my life?"

I was dating a man that the Lord said "no" to. I was not married, I had just taken the bar exam, and I was in a high risk pregnancy. I was also arrogant, self-centered, foolish, and prideful. I did not give God the glory for what He had given me because I was stiff-necked, rebellious, and hypocritical—having a form of godliness, but denying the power thereof. I did not fear God. Yes, I went to church, but I was fornicating. I did not have a relationship with God. Of a truth, I was not even saved. If I knew or even understood what God's purpose for me was, I would not have spent so many years outside of His will. Then again, who's to say if I knew my purpose, I would not have tried to continue under my own strength.

Later, I learned from my pastor that the root word of salvation is *to salvage*. Salvage is the act of saving or rescuing property in danger; it is property saved from destruction in a calamity; it is something extracted (as from rubbish) as valuable or useful.[1] There should be a rejoicing and continuous thanksgiving that God loves us, that He has not lost love for us, that He does not want us to be lost.

So, although I had given "lip service" and, at one point, accepted Jesus as my personal savior, I had never given "life service"—the conversion never took place, there was no true repentance, and there was no change. So, in fact,

---

[1] "Salvage." *Merriam-Webster.com*. 2012. http://www.merriam-webster.com (28 May 2012).

I'm not sure if I was *ever* saved, especially since my life did not align with Christ. Additionally, the things that were reflected in my life were not the will of God for my life. I was not walking in God's purposes for my life.

My purpose: for me to understand that Jesus didn't come to bring a religion, but to introduce the Kingdom of God, which was there from the beginning. I am an Ambassador for Christ (2 Cor. 5:20), a royal priesthood (1 Peter 2:9), and heir and joint heir with Christ (Rom 8:17); a citizen in God's kingdom. The Lord, who is Adonai, which means owner, owns everything. The earth is the Lord's, and the fullness thereof; the world, and they that dwell therein (Psalm 24:1). As owner, He owns even me. So if God is the owner of everything and he owns me, then my purpose is to do God's will. My purpose is to be obedient and submitted to the Sovereign King. My purpose is to worship the Lord, which is what I was created to do. My purpose is to teach the same thing Jesus taught—the Kingdom of God!

I did not, and could not, understand that until I was walking in the purpose that God had pre-ordained for me, I would continue to fall. I would continue to fail. As long I was walking in a purpose that I had chosen for myself, I could never prosper; my goals would never come to fruition. It was as if I was trying to live someone else's life, not the life God had intended for me. Consequently, things never really seemed to work out. Although I was a dedicated worker, had well-paying jobs, worked for some very good companies, I would eventually get laid off. I was often overlooked, but more significantly, I just was never happy or satisfied. It was as if I could not fit in; I never found my place.

I did not know who I was. My identity was wrapped up in stuff. I owned my own house, car, and etc., but I was trying to be a "people-pleaser". There were a lot of people in my circle, but I still felt empty. I could not really fit in because I was never really a part. I had made idols out of things, when the Lord commanded us to not have other gods before Him. (Exodus 20:3)

> *All who fashion idols are nothing, and the things they delight in do not profit.* (Isaiah 44:9, ESV)

As the Lord drew me to Himself, He removed not only people from my life, but the things I had accrued without Him: houses, car, marriage, and children.

When my marriage failed, I felt lost. I could not talk to anyone; it was as if I was in a void. I was screaming, but no one could hear. The more I fought, the more things were taken away, to the point that I had to surrender myself to God. Surrender was very difficult at first, especially since I was trained to be very independent, self reliant, headstrong, and full of pride. I realized that the thing I was fighting, the person that I was fighting, was God who was the one who would save me. This is when He started changing my life around. Slowly, but surely, I started to really understand the relationship I had to have with God; and the relationship He wanted to have with me. Then God started to rebuild my life and this was not an easy process. In fact, I'm still in the rebuilding phase—God is continuing to restore my life. He is not finished with me because I do not know what my final purpose is, or rather, what God's final plan is for me.

Some of the things I "lost", God allowed me to regain. Today, I have a better relationship with my children. Every single day I try to better myself, to understand, and to show them the loving kindness that I may not have shown them when I was going through my own trials. I thought I would never have a relationship with a man again, especially after the pain, the suffering, and the betrayal. We can all understand what it is like to have a bad relationship, whether it's with a spouse or someone you were dating. It can incapacitate you or make you feel or think that you will die.

But, with prayer, deliverance, and time, God sent the man that He had ordained for me. We met, we married, and we are building a life together. God restored the love, the joy, the laughter, and the peace. I am happy, thankful and grateful. I love the Lord with all my heart, mind, soul and strength because had God not loved me first and rescued me, I would have not known Him for myself.

As for the law, I do not practice law, but I use my degree, my skills and what I've learned to consult. I could not go back to corporate America because corporate America could not satisfy me the way that I thought it would. I've written a book and am currently writing the second. I use the book as a way to reach out to those who have walked the path that I have walked or who are about to walk the path. Currently, I am using the book as form of a ministry, speaking to young people, and encouraging them to know and love themselves.

God has a sense of humor. In addition to the fact that His ways are not our ways, His thoughts higher than our thoughts (Isaiah 58:8-9), God knew how to draw me to Himself, to align me into His will. As I reflect back, at first it was music—God used the desire of my heart, recording a CD, to draw me and deliver me. Then, He used the task of writing a book as a form of deliverance and forgiveness. But as I stated, God has a sense of humor, because when God called me to preach His word, I laughed with trepidation. I said, "God, me? I am so unworthy Lord. I know where you've brought me from. Are you sure you want to use me?" I am not sure all of the details of where I am going to preach or how I am going to preach, but God knows all things. When afforded the opportunity, I realize the Holy Spirit will let me know where I should go and give me the Words to say.

To whom am I to preach? I still don't know what my life is all about, but God has called me to preach. I make myself available and at His appointed time He gives the message pouring forth from the heart of the Father to the people, so that the people leave knowing the heart of the Father. To God be the Glory!

I remember after I published the first book, the Holy Spirit would repeatedly say to me, "It is not about the book." Yet I didn't understand. So when the Lord called me to preach, He gave me more clarity. I realized it was not about the book! The book was a tool to prepare me, just like recording the CD was a tool to draw me and deliver me. God is awesome!

Philippians 1:6 says that He who begins a good work in you is faithful to complete it. Although I do not know the years and what lies ahead of me, I do know that God is faithful to complete the investment that He'd placed in me from the beginning. God knew us before the foundations of the world (Eph 1:3-5); even before we were in our mothers' wombs (Jeremiah 1:5). God covered us and fashioned all of our days (Psalms 139:13-16). God saw and knew the purpose and plans for my life (Jeremiah 29:11). This fact brings me much joy and comfort.

The Prosperity

First and foremost, I have a relationship with God. I have a relationship with my family. I have a relationship with friends, some from the past, and some from the present.

Overall, I believe my life is on the right track. Daily I strive to keep God first, follow His rules, obey His Word, walk uprightly before Him, show love, have joy, be thankful and grateful, abide by the rules of His kingdom, and repent when I fail.

Now, I am ever so diligent in giving God the glory for everything; especially, for all that He's done, is doing, and is going to do. For all that I am and all that I have is because of Him, and I humbly stay before Him to make sure that my life is lining up with His Word.

As I consider my journey I could not appreciate God's love when in my sin, nor did I love Him back. I then met God as my Savior and opened my heart to invite Jesus to reside within me through the person of the Holy Spirit. When I was baptized by the Holy Spirit, He became my Counselor and my Guide. When I began to yield, He then became my Deliverer. Once the conversion took place, He became my Lord. When I started learning about the Kingdom of God, He became my Sovereign King.

I never understood, nor did I apply the scripture in Matthew 6:33: *But seek ye first the kingdom of God, and his righteousness; and all these things shall be added unto you.* It was not until I was willing to give up everything gained "without God," that I was able to be content, no matter the situation, and that I was able to give God the Glory, and that I was able to "gain" God. The blessing is the "Blessor." Having a relationship with Him is the increase; seeking the Kingdom of God and His righteousness is the increase; receiving the manifestation of my purpose is the increase. I am no longer poor, but rich because the King of Kings, who owns the entire earth is my Father, and my Sovereign King. He is true to His promise: "But seek ye first God's Kingdom, governing authority, His rule, His dominion, and the very act of Him ruling, day to day, moment by moment; and live Right, the way God lived, according to God's way of doing and being right, having compassion, giving everyone their just due, operating with mercy and justice, seeing people as He sees them; with provision, giving others of what you have, part of your resources, as God gives you His resources; and everything else will be added unto you."[2] I give God the Glory!

---

[2] Dr. Leonard Robinson, Pastor, Kingdom Vision Ministries International.

I am from the Bronx. In a rap that came out in the late 80's, while I was growing up, there is a line that says, "It ain't where you're from, it's where you're at."[3] Those words have never been more true, but in Christ. It's not the fact that I am from the Bronx, or that I am not from somewhere else, or that I came from a certain race or was born of certain parents or am from a certain socio-economic background: but it is who I am in Christ and what I do for Christ that has any value and will last for eternity.

---

[3] Eric B. & Rakim, *I Know You Got Soul, Paid in Full* Album (4th & B'way, 1987).

Chapter 10 / Synopsis
Alfreda Bradford

*Beloved, I wish **above all things** that thou may prosper and be in health, even as thy soul prospers. (3 John 2)*

God's intentions pertaining to his children are not a secret. Above all things, first of all, He desires that you live a life of prosperity. He wants you to experience prosperity and increase in every area of your life – your mind, your body, your health, your wealth, your relationships, and etc. However, your good success is contingent on your soul's wellbeing; on the salvation of your soul and your hunger pertaining to the things that belong to Him.

You are a spirit made in the image of God, you possess a soul (mind, will and emotions), and you live in a body. Many are aiming at accumulating material benefits with no regard to the condition of their spirit man—in God's economy, this is backwards.

Lack, shortage, brokenness, devastation, sickness, disease, poverty, and etc. are all the byproducts of sin, which Jesus destroyed when He was resurrected from the dead. Jesus completely fulfilled His mission and thereby we have an inheritance to probate an abundant life, mindset and lifestyle, by faith. These are real manifestations which increase incrementally, but it begins in the spirit, where everything else begins.

Faith in Jesus gives us access to start over again, regardless of where you've been, how long you've been there, what you've done and what you've experienced. Even for those of you who have experienced what you consider to be a good life, an immersion of God's glory and His presence will position you to live a life of absolute victory moving "From Poverty to Prosperity" – from unrest to exceeding peace. He is the King of Peace. Jesus is Lord.

Taste and see that the Lord is good!

APPENDIX

Salvation

Reasons to Evangelize

Evangelism is not simply an option for Christians. It is not a responsibility reserved only for those who seemingly have the gift of evangelism. Evangelism is a mandate for every believer and an essential element for living the Christian life. The Bible gives several reasons and motivations for Christians to evangelize, and among them are these: the commandment of Christ (Matthew 28:19-20), the knowledge that sinners require a Savior, and that evangelism is a way to show our faith and love toward Christ as well as others. So, join us and become a fisher of men.

How Are We Saved?

Whosoever believes that Jesus is the Christ is born of God; and every one that loveth Him that begat loveth Him also that is begotten of Him (1 John 5:1). The way that you are saved is by believing that Jesus is the Christ.

Acts 16:31 says: "Believe on the Lord Jesus Christ, and thou shalt be saved, and they house." Believing in the Lord Jesus saves us.

James 2:18-19 says, "Yeah, a man may say, "Thou has faith, and I have works: show me they faith without they works, and I will show thee my faith by my works. Thou believest that there is one God; thou doest well: the devils also believe, and tremble." The word "believe" means to have trust and commitment in something.

Ephesians 2:8-9 makes it abundantly clear: "For by grace are ye saved through faith; and that not of yourselves: it is the gift of God: Not of works, lest any man should boast." Self cannot save. Works cannot save. God saves us by His grace through our faith in Christ.

You may think this is too simplistic, bit if you were to ask most people if they are saved, you will hear them start talking about themselves and their works. Those who are counting on their own works to get them into heaven are not saved.

Every person is dead in their sins if they have not trusted Jesus Christ as their Lord and Savior. Grace is the unmerited love and favor God shows to sinners. God loves us when we are unlovely. He does not love you for what you have done. He loves you out of His grace.

Now, Satan does not want you to understand that. He wants you to think salvation depends on what you do. But, that's a trap because you will always be wondering if you've done enough. Salvation depends not on what you do, but on what God does for you. "And if by grace, then is it no more of works: otherwise grace is no more grace. But if it be of works, then it is no more grace: otherwise work is no more work" (Romans 11:6).

Salvation is not part grace and part works. It is ALL GRACE.

About the Author

Alfreda Bradford

Alfreda Bradford is a Kingdom Coach and a servant of the true and living God. She is a sought after, licensed, and ordained Minister of the Gospel of Jesus Christ, serving as a Pastor-Evangelist. She serves faithfully to promote the Kingdom of God and God's purpose and people. Over the years, her Divine calling, in addition to her variety of gifts and willingness to serve, has placed her within the area she was most needed, including the office of Youth Pastor.

Evangelist Bradford is the Visionary of "Life Word Jesus Ministries" with a Mission to inspire, empower, and elevate the mindset of youth and adults. We equip individuals to shift their focus toward becoming capable leaders within their communities and spheres of influence.

The ministry holds monthly Kingdom Leadership Responsibility Conferences wherein the audience is challenged to explore the art and science of leadership. Through these events, the "art" of leadership is promoted as seen in the discovery of creativity and growth; alongside the "science" of leadership where effective tools are developed. These tools contribute to growth and success in the areas of family, faith, business, civil service, or wherever a person serves in society.

In addition to her role as a church leader (uninterrupted since January 1, 2010), she currently hosts, "Life Word Jesus Prayer Conference Call Ministry". This call takes place at 5:45 a.m. (EST) every morning, 6 days a week, Monday through Saturday. This ministry offers prayer, inspiration and encouragement through God's Word to individuals around the globe.

Alfreda is a published author, inventor and business woman. A previous television personality, she currently hosts a weekly internet Radio show interviewing leaders across the nation discussing the full spectrum of Leadership.

As an entrepreneur, Alfreda Bradford is the founder and CEO of *Let Us Talk Wealth, LLC*, a business development consultant company. In this role, she hosted a weekly television show on Saturdays and Sundays called *Let's Talk Wealth*. Here she challenged her viewing audience to think outside of the box in order to achieve uncommon success.

A servant leader, Alfreda is a self-motivated multi-million dollar producer, and previous real estate broker with over 30 years of experience. An inspired writer since elementary school, recognized for her writing style and poetry, she authored *"The Good Things in Life"* in 2005, and recently completed her autobiography *"She Was Me"*. Her third book is soon to be released. www.alfredabradford.com

Ms. Bradford, known affectionately and professionally as "Alfreda B.", is single and the mother of 3 beautiful, gifted, talented and self-employed daughters. She is also the grandmother of 4 and a mother-in-law.

She is currently completing her doctoral degree at Accelerated School of Christian Ministry International.

About the Contributors

Tonya Patterson, is a multi-talented counselor, seminar speaker, author, and founder of Saved, Single, and Sanctified Ministries, which encourages Holy Spirit led relationships. She also plays the piano, sings at churches, and serves as Inspirational Reader/Speaker. She has one grown son.

Letitia Alexander was born and raised in Dayton Ohio, and is the mother of two lovely daughters along with a son in-law and three wonderful grandchildren. Letitia has a background in communication and education, and has been an avid student of scripture for over 10 years.

Tanya Norwood is the founder of *Today Realize Your Dreams* which was created to show individuals how to take control of their own destiny utilizing the goal setting process. A speaker for over 20 years, Tanya presents on various topics including the goal setting process and her own personal story. Tanya has been featured on television, radio, and in print; and she has been mentored by motivational speaker and trainer, Les Brown. Tanya's stories, "Show Me How to Live", published in The Queens

Legacy and "What Becomes of a Breaking Heart", published in The Fragmented Heart Healers are written to inspire, encourage and empower individuals to live the abundant life promised them in the Word of God. *tnorwood.legalshieldassociate.com*

Shawntrell Sherrod, through the Prophecy of God is a ReadyWriter and has published three books with many more on the way. She has several inventions and is pressing on in Faith and obedience and has begun recording her ministry program of "Preach: Be a Voice Not an Echo." *wwwdotmh.webs.com*

Dr. Inetta Jenkins-Cooper founded WomenNPower International Ministry Network in 2004, and serves as its CEO. Soon after it was launched MenNPower Ministry Network and TeensNPower Ministry Network were born. Simultaneously, she serves as CEO of NPower Media Group of Atlanta and is the publisher of NPower Magazine Online. Dr. Cooper also produces and hosts her own show *View from the Pew*. She holds a Masters in Business and Ethics and received a Doctorate of Religious Studies from Saint Thomas Christian Theologian Seminary, Jacksonville Florida. She answered the call to preach in 2003 and was ordained as a Pastor and Elder under the Deliverance Ministries HQ Church in South Carolina. www.womennpower.com

Carmelo Colon, Jr. is a professional hair stylist in Jenkintown, PA. He has many gifts and abilities. He loves the Lord and God's people. He is single and desires to promote the Kingdom of God and fulfill God's divine purpose for his life.

Brother Peter Edwin is the author of *"Deliverance through Confessions"* and *"Step by Step to the Lord"*, soon to be released. He is the President and CEO of *Quit Violence International*, a non-profit organization located in Pennsylvania and New York. A graduate of Defense Acquisition University in Virginia, and George Washington University, he works as a Certified Specialist Counselor for Domestic Violence. He is happily married to Gloria. www.quitviolenceintl.org

J.B. Tremont A writer who balances humor with reality, Tremont offers a fresh perspective by giving practical advice utilizing biblical principles. Formally trained as an attorney, she holds a Jurist Doctorate degree and a

Bachelors of Science degree in Labor Relations. Although she does not practice law, she utilizes her legal training as a consultant to other entrepreneurs with their business start-up and development. J.B. Tremont is the author of *"He Loves You, Not: A Commonsense Guide to What NOT to do in Relationships"*. Presently, Tremont continues to write, is a Minister of the Gospel of Jesus Christ, conducts workshops and lectures, consults, and is an entrepreneur running multiple businesses. *www.jbtremont.com*

www.ingramcontent.com/pod-product-compliance
Lightning Source LLC
LaVergne TN
LVHW051605070426
835507LV00021B/2781